Study Skills

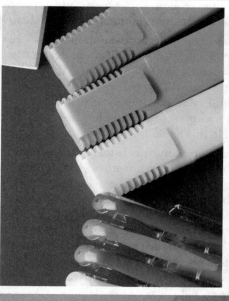

Publisher
The Goodheart-Willcox Company, Inc.
Tinley Park, IL
www.g-w.com

Preface

Study skills are the strategies a student applies to learning that helps facilitate understanding and retention of knowledge. These are the skills that become good habits and enable an individual to become efficient, solve problems, and apply critical-thinking skills. In today's competitive academic environment, possession of well-developed study skills can be the competitive edge a student needs for college and career success.

Study Skills presents essential study strategies in an easy to understand format. Fourteen short, concise lessons provide information that will prepare students to become active learners. A chapter-opening pretest sets the stage for the content that follows. End-of-chapter activities provide opportunities for self-assessment as well as additional practice activities on the G-W Learning Companion Website.

Learning how to become an active learner and focused student is the first step toward personal success. Presented in a brief, concise, and easy-to-use text, students will learn the basic study skills needed for classroom success. Suitable for any class or discipline, each chapter can be used as a supplemental discussion tool about the development of study habits or as an independent assignment. When the course has concluded, the text can serve as a personal reference for personal, academic, and career success.

Additional Resources

The G-W Learning Companion Website is a free student resource that provides additional study materials in an interactive electronic format. Activity files for the skills practice activities at the end of each chapter may be downloaded and completed for additional practice. Also included on the website are pretests and vocabulary activities that complement selected chapters. The website is located at **www.g-wlearning.com/careereducation/**

G-W's instructor resources include everything you need to utilize *Study Skills* in your classroom. A variety of materials are provided on the Instructor's Resource CD to help you make the most of information needed to teach each chapter, such as lesson plans, answer keys, and instructional strategies.

Angeles College
3440 Wilshire Blvd., Suite 310
Los Angeles, CA 90010
Tel. (213) 487-2211

Acknowledgments

Goodheart-Willcox Publisher would like to thank the following individuals for their honest and valuable input in the development of the first edition of *Study Skills*.

Neoka Marple Apple, PhD, Instructor, Adjunct Faculty, Social and Behavioral Science, St. Petersburg College, St. Petersburg, FL

Sophie Lampard Dennis, Associate Professor, Education, Landmark College, Putney, VT

Cathy Hamilton, Instructor, Engineering Drawing and Design, Prosser Career Education Center, New Albany, IN

Robert André LaFleur, Professor, History and Anthropology, Beloit College, Beloit, WI

Court Merrigan, Coordinator, Center for Tutoring and Learning, Eastern Wyoming College, Torrington, WY

Ashley Stich, Instructor, Residential Readying Faculty, Mesa Community College, Mesa, AZ

Paige Talbot, Instructor, English, South Seattle College, Seattle, WA

Brief Contents

Contents

Focus on Study Habits

Study Skills will help your students apply strategies to learning that will help them facilitate understanding and retention of knowledge. In order to become successful in college and career, it is necessary to develop study habits that will help them become efficient, learn to solve problems, and apply critical-thinking skills. Possession of well-developed study skills can be the competitive edge a student needs for academic success.

The unique approach to this text presents content in a format that is condensed, to the point, and can be completed in a brief amount of time. The easy-to-read style and meaningful applications introduce behaviors for successful interactions with instructors as well as classmates.

Just the Basics

Each chapter introduces basic study skills as recommended by instructors. The topics covered are some of the most requested essential study skills that can help students become active learners and develop habits that will last a lifetime.

Learning Outcomes

At the beginning of each chapter, learning outcomes define the goals that will be accomplished while reading the chapter. Each goal is aligned with the content headings, as well as with the summary at the end of the chapter. The alignment of learning outcomes provides a logical flow through each page of the content so that students may build on individual knowledge as they progress through the chapters.

Before You Read

Each chapter begins with a pretest for an opportunity for students to evaluate their prior knowledge of the study skill that will be introduced. This sets the stage for content to come in each chapter.

APPENDIX A

Portfolio Development

Portfolio Development activities provide guidance for creating a personal portfolio to use when exploring volunteer, education and training, and career opportunities. This process requires that you self-reflect on personal accomplishments and skills as you create documentation for final presentation. Completing these activities will help you prepare a professional product for the job-application process, giving you a head start on your career search in an increasingly competitive workforce.

Lesson 1: Overview

When applying for a job, a volunteer position, or entry into an educational institution, one way to demonstrate your qualifications is to present a portfolio to the interviewer. A *portfolio* is a selection of related materials that you collect and organize to demonstrate your job qualifications, skills, and talents. For example, a certification showing you have completed Microsoft Office Specialist training could help you get a job at a local newspaper. A portfolio is a *dynamic document*, which means it should be reviewed and updated on a regular basis.

Visual artists and communication professionals have historically presented portfolios of their creative work when seeking jobs or admission to educational institutions. However, portfolios are now used in many professions. It is helpful to research and identify which type is appropriate for the industry in which you are applying for a position.

Commonly used formats for a portfolio are print and electronic. Job seekers will need copies of a print portfolio, as well as an electronic version, when applying for a position.

A *print portfolio* is a hard-copy version that can be carried to an interview. It can be presented in a three-ring binder with divider tabs or any other method that works for you.

An *electronic portfolio* is a digital version of a print portfolio. It can be saved to cloud-based storage services, flash drives, or CDs. There are many creative ways to present a digital portfolio. One option is to create an electronic presentation with slides for each item. Another option is to place the files on a CD. Websites also work well for presenting an electronic portfolio. The method you choose should allow the viewer to navigate and find items easily.

As you collect materials for your portfolio, you will need an effective strategy to keep the items clean, safe, and organized for assembly at the appropriate time. Structure and organization are important when working on an on-going project that includes multiple pieces. Never include an original document in a portfolio. Photocopy each document that you want to include and file the original in a safe place for future reference.

A large manila envelope works well to keep hard copies of documents, photos, awards, and other items safe. File folders also work well.

1. Research *Types of Portfolios* and select the one that is most appropriate for you and your career goals.

2. Consider and plan for the technology that might be needed for creating and scanning documents for an electronic portfolio. You may need access to desktop-publishing software, scan-

---

SUMMARY

- **(LO 1-1) Explain the concept of study skills.**
  Study skills are the strategies a person applies to learning. They are how you approach learning, select processes that work for you, and eliminate distractions that hinder you from your goals.
- **(LO 1-2) Identify three personal behaviors that can help a person develop study skills.**
  Examples of personal behaviors that help an individual develop study skills are having a positive attitude, self-confidence, and focus.
- **(LO 1-3) Cite the steps of the decision-making process.**
  The decision-making process involves five steps: define the problem, gather information, choose the best alternative, act on the decision, and evaluate the solution or decision.
- **(LO 1-4) List examples of pre-study tips.**
  Examples of pre-study tips are to avoid multitasking, turn off digital devices, and take care of your personal well-being.
- **(LO 1-5) Summarize academic integrity.**
  Academic integrity is the demonstration of honesty and responsibility in completion of academic work and performance as a student. Being unprepared or copying answers on a test is unacceptable behavior. In addition, presenting information in a report as yours when you really copied material that belongs to another person is plagiarism and will not contribute to you earning an education needed for future employment. From the first day of class, realize that your job is to learn, make good grades, and get a well-rounded education. Communicate with your instructor, attend class, and be an ethical individual.

GLOSSARY TERMS

Visit the G-W Learning companion website at **www.g-wlearning.com/careereducation/** to review the following glossary terms.

skill
study skills
soft skills
transferable skills
attitude
self-confidence
self-talk
focus

decision-making
critical-thinking skills
academic integrity
plagiarism
ethics
morals
integrity

REVIEW

1. Discuss study skills.

2. List three examples of study skills.

3. Identify examples of personal behaviors that are needed to develop good study skills.

Appendices

Appendix A, Portfolio Development, provides detailed information for creating a career portfolio for academic and professional use. An appendix is also included for punctuation, capitalization, and number usage. Appendix B highlights grammar mechanics and examples for reference as students complete writing assignments.

End-of-Chapter Content

End-of-chapter material provides opportunity for review and application of concepts.

- A concise **Summary** reiterates the learning outcomes and provides a brief review of the content for student reference.

- **Glossary Terms** identifies important study skills terms covered in the chapter and listed in the end-of-text glossary.

- **Review** questions highlight basic concepts presented in the chapter so students can evaluate understanding of the material.

- **Critical Thinking** activities provide an opportunity for self-reflection so students can relate the topics to their personal lives.

- **Internet** exercises provide additional research opportunities for greater understanding of selected concepts discussed in the chapter.

- **Skills Practice** activities provide an opportunity for students to engage in hands-on application of the content to perfect their study skills.

G-W Learning Companion Website

The G-W Learning Companion Website is a free resource that provides additional study materials in an interactive electronic format. Activity files for the skills practice activities at the end of each chapter may be downloaded and completed for additional practice. Also included on the website are pretests, post-tests, and vocabulary activities that complement selected chapters. The website is located at **www.g-wlearning.com/careereducation/**

Developing Study Skills

Monkey Business Images/Shutterstock.com

BEFORE YOU READ

Before you begin reading this chapter, see what you already know about study skills by taking a pretest. The pretest is available at **www.g-wlearning.com/careereducation/**

LEARNING OUTCOMES

On completion of this chapter, prepare to:

1-1 Explain the concept of study skills.

1-2 Identify three personal behaviors that can help a person develop study skills.

1-3 Cite the steps of the decision-making process.

1-4 List examples of pre-study tips.

1-5 Summarize academic integrity.

Self-confidence is being certain and secure about one's own abilities and judgment.

Norman Pogson/Shutterstock.com

Study Skills

In order to be successful in your academic career and your personal life, it will be necessary for you to develop study skills. A **skill** is something an individual does well. **Study skills** are the strategies a person applies to effective learning. They are how you approach learning, select processes that work for you, and eliminate distractions that hinder you from achieving your goals.

Study skills become good habits that help you become efficient, solve problems, and apply critical-thinking skills. They can make you a more attentive listener, better reader, and more efficient note taker. Practicing and developing these skills will help you become a better student. If your grades are suffering, developing good study skills can help you improve them. If your grades are average, improving your study skills can bring your grades up a notch. Examples of study skills are listed in Figure 1-1.

Study skills are classified as *soft skills*. **Soft skills** are the skills used to communicate and work well with others. They are considered essential **transferable skills**, which are skills that help an individual find a job, perform well in the workplace, and gain success in a job or career.

Once you master study skills, you will apply them in your day-to-day life because they are not subject specific. For example, you will apply study skills as you prepare for the test to get your driver's license. You will also apply them to learn how to use a computer or your smartphone. Many study skills also transfer into employability skills you will need when you finish school and start a career.

Developing Study Skills

As you progress through school, you will value possessing the knowledge of how to get the most out of your study time. Every person studies differently, and strategies that work well for one person might not be effective for another.

Through experience, you will learn how to develop the study skills that work best for you. Just as importantly, you will learn to disregard the less effective ones. The sooner you begin the process, the sooner you will experience success. The journey begins with having a positive attitude, self-confidence, and focus.

Figure 1-1 Study skills are the various strategies a person applies to learning.

Study Skills

- decision-making
- time management
- organization
- study environment
- avoid distractions
- comprehension
- active reading
- vocabulary building
- active listening
- note taking
- active learning
- test taking
- research
- stress management

Goodheart-Willcox Publisher

Attitude

Attitude is how personal thoughts or feelings affect a person's outward behavior. It is a combination of how a person feels, what he or she thinks, and what he or she does. Attitude is how an individual sees himself or herself, as well as how he or she perceives others.

Positive attitudes often play an important role in determining academic performance. An individual with a *positive attitude* is optimistic and looks at the upside of a situation rather than the downside. Optimists learn from experiences, accurately identify problems, and try to offer solutions rather than complaints. Having a positive attitude is the first step to learning how to study.

A good attitude about studying includes a sense of responsibility for your own learning. You will be a lifelong learner. As a *lifelong learner*, you will look for opportunities to learn information for personal and professional use. Some of your learning will come from formal schooling. Other learning will come from life experiences and your desire to improve your mind and your well-being.

Self-Confidence

An important element of an individual's success is self-confidence. **Self-confidence** is being certain and secure about one's own abilities and judgment. People with self-confidence believe in their ability to perform or make something positive happen in a situation.

A person's self-confidence is affected by his or her self-talk. **Self-talk** is the practice of talking to oneself, either silently or aloud. This is how most individuals sort through information. It often includes reinforcement about one's appearance, personal qualities, and belief in one's self. The more you believe in yourself, the more others will believe in you. If you are confident you can develop study skills, you will be able to succeed.

Focus

Most importantly, developing good study skills requires you to focus. To **focus** means to pay close attention to something. In order to pay attention, you have to recognize the importance of what you are doing so you fully understand the value of the task.

If you are learning how to study, the importance of the task is to help you be more productive as a student and person. When listening to your instructor lecture, the importance is to learn about the topic being discussed. When reading assigned texts or material, the importance is to learn the facts and details that are being presented. Recognizing the importance of the task adds value and clarity.

Decision-Making Process

As a student, you will be challenged every day to make decisions to solve a situation that arises. These situations can range from deciding which class to take to narrowing down a topic for a research paper. It is important not to become overwhelmed especially if time is a factor.

Decision-making is the process of solving a problem or situation. The process includes choosing a course of action after evaluating available information and weighing the costs, benefits, and consequences of alternative actions.

Decision-making involves critical-thinking skills. **Critical-thinking skills** are skills that provide the ability to analyze and interpret a situation and make reasonable judgments and decisions. When you apply critical-thinking skills, you try to eliminate emotions and be open-minded about the possibilities. Then, a solution or process can be applied so that a productive action can be taken.

Applying systematic decision-making is a necessary study skill. There are five general steps to this process, as illustrated in Figure 1-2.

1. *Define the problem.* A clear idea of the problem must be formulated in order to find the best approach. If the problem is too broad, you will not be able to accurately address the issue and find a solution. If there is a specific goal in mind, make sure it's measurable and timely in order to know whether you've achieved it at the end of the process.

2. *Gather information.* Gather information in order to base your decision on data and facts. You need to know what information is relevant to solving the problem at hand.

3. *Choose the best alternative.* After considering all potential solutions, the one that best fits the situation can be selected. It may be a single alternative or some combination of alternatives.

4. *Act on the decision.* Once a decision is made, it should be executed. What steps must be done to make this happen?

5. *Evaluate the solution or decision.* After time has passed, the solution can be analyzed to determine if it was the correct course of action.

Applying systematic decision-making is a skill that can help you throughout your life. Learning to apply critical-thinking skills and problem solve can help you in most situations that you will encounter.

Pre-Study Tips

Before you begin studying, there are several things you can do to prepare yourself to make the most out of your study time. Some general study tips include the following:

- Avoid multitasking when there is something important, such as studying, that needs your immediate and undivided attention. Multitasking can serve a purpose in the right situation. It is difficult to pay attention and do your best, however, if you are trying to do two things at once. Decide to focus exclusively on the task at hand.

- Turn off your digital devices when you need to give your full attention to a task. You will hear this advice frequently as you progress through this text. It is aimed to help you avoid distractions in all aspects of your school and personal life.

Figure 1-2 Decision-making is the process of solving a problem or situation by choosing a course of action after evaluating the possible solutions.

Goodheart-Willcox Publisher

Above all, good study habits begin with your personal well-being. If your body is not healthy and alert, it will be difficult for you to pay attention. The following are some hints for keeping yourself well and ready to learn.

- Rest is crucial. On average, you should be getting between eight and ten hours of sleep each night. *Fatigue*, or sleepiness, can keep you from being productive at school, at your job, or in your personal life.

- Hydration is necessary and can be accomplished by drinking water and limiting sugar and caffeine.

- Balanced meals are important, and excessive snacking should be avoided. Eating right can keep your body healthy and your mind sharp, instead of feeling hyper, sluggish, or distracted.

There are multiple study tips you will learn as you progress through the lessons in this text that will help you have a positive attitude toward studying, have confidence in your ability to study effectively, and focus on tasks at hand.

Academic Integrity

Academic integrity is the demonstration of honesty and responsibility in completion of academic work and performance as a student. As a student, you attend school to earn an education that will help you in your future personal life and career. Being unprepared or copying answers on a test is unacceptable behavior. In addition, presenting information in a report as yours when you really copied material that belongs to another person is plagiarism and will not contribute to you earning an education needed for future employment. **Plagiarism** is claiming another person's material as your own, which is both unethical and illegal.

Cheating is a violation of academic integrity.

Constantine Pankin/Shutterstock.com

Above all, demonstrate a sense of ethics at all times. **Ethics** are the moral principles that direct a person's behaviors. **Morals** are an individual's ideas of what is right and wrong. **Integrity** is the honesty of a person's actions. Educational institutions expect, and require, students to perform in an ethical manner when taking tests, writing reports, and completing assignments.

Strive to be a good student. From the first day of class, realize that your job is to learn, achieve good grades, and earn a well-rounded education. The following actions can help you be successful in your studies.

- Communicate with your instructor and be clear on what he or she expects from you as a student.

- Ask your instructor for contact information if you should need after class help. Your instructor may have office hours or prefer e-mail correspondence when you have questions.

- Read the course outline or syllabus that you are given. Request clarification on anything that you do not understand or is not clear.

- Confirm the name of the text and other materials that are needed for the class.

- Attend every class, and be on time. There will be times when you are ill or an emergency arises. When this happens be prepared to make up the time and meet with your instructor to find out what you missed.

- Be polite and use good manners with your fellow students.

- Raise your hand when you want to contribute in class. Avoid interrupting others when they are talking.

Be positive and learn to appreciate the privilege of earning an education. Attending school is one of the best times of your life. Enjoy it, and be the best you can be.

SUMMARY

- **(LO 1-1) Explain the concept of study skills.**
  Study skills are the strategies a person applies to learning. They are how you approach learning, select processes that work for you, and eliminate distractions that hinder you from your goals.
- **(LO 1-2) Identify three personal behaviors that can help a person develop study skills.**
  Examples of personal behaviors that help an individual develop study skills are having a positive attitude, self-confidence, and focus.
- **(LO 1-3) Cite the steps of the decision-making process.**
  The decision-making process involves five steps: define the problem, gather information, choose the best alternative, act on the decision, and evaluate the solution or decision.
- **(LO 1-4) List examples of pre-study tips.**
  Examples of pre-study tips are to avoid multitasking, turn off digital devices, and take care of your personal well-being.
- **(LO 1-5) Summarize academic integrity.**
  Academic integrity is the demonstration of honesty and responsibility in completion of academic work and performance as a student. Being unprepared or copying answers on a test is unacceptable behavior. In addition, presenting information in a report as yours when you really copied material that belongs to another person is plagiarism and will not contribute to you earning an education needed for future employment. From the first day of class, realize that your job is to learn, make good grades, and get a well-rounded education. Communicate with your instructor, attend class, and be an ethical individual.

GLOSSARY TERMS

Visit the G-W Learning companion website at **www.g-wlearning.com/careereducation/** to review the following glossary terms.

skill	decision-making
study skills	critical-thinking skills
soft skills	academic integrity
transferable skills	plagiarism
attitude	ethics
self-confidence	morals
self-talk	integrity
focus	

REVIEW

1. Discuss study skills.

2. List three examples of study skills.

3. Identify examples of personal behaviors that are needed to develop good study skills.

4. Explain how someone with a positive attitude views the world.

5. Describe self-talk and its role in a person's self-confidence.

6. In order to focus and pay attention, what must a person do?

7. What happens when critical-thinking skills are applied?

8. State the steps of the decision-making process.

9. Briefly state examples of general pre-study skills.

10. Summarize academic integrity.

CRITICAL THINKING

1. Define the importance of study skills for your academic success.

2. Why are you considered a lifelong learner?

3. In addition to the pre-study tips discussed in this chapter, how do you prepare yourself physically and mentally for studying?

4. Describe how others view you as a student. Would they say you are a good student or someone who needs improvement? Discuss your actions that influence their opinion.

5. Summarize what academic integrity means to you.

INTERNET ACTIVITY

Habits of Highly Successful Students. Students who have a successful educational experience learned early in their school career how to be a successful student. Conduct an Internet search for *habits of highly successful students*. Evaluate what you discovered and how you can apply the information to your personal life.

Academic Integrity. Many schools have a code of academic integrity that students are obligated to follow. Conduct an Internet search for *academic integrity definition*. Summarize what you learned and discuss why this behavior is important for your future career. If your school has a code of academic integrity, compare it to your Internet findings.

SKILLS PRACTICE

Visit the G-W Learning companion website at **www.g-wlearning.com/careereducation/** to access and complete the following study skills practice activities:

Study Skills Activity 1-1 Self-Assessment. Assessing your personal study skills will help you determine your strengths and weaknesses. Open the 1-1 file, and complete the assessment to evaluate your current study skills.

Study Skills Activity 1-2 The Decision-Making Process. Applying systematic decision-making is a skill that can help you throughout your life. Identify a decision or problem that you need to solve in the near future. Open the 1-2 file, state your decision or problem, and apply the decision-making process to come to a solution.

Study Skills Activity 1-3 First Day of Class Checklist. Being prepared for the semester is an important first step to establishing good study skills. On the first day of class, start with a checklist of what will be required. Open the 1-3 file, and customize it to fit your needs. Use this list for the first day of each class in which you are enrolled.

CHAPTER 2

Identifying Your Learning Style

Andrey_Popov/Shutterstock.com

BEFORE YOU READ

Before you begin reading this chapter, see what you already know about learning styles by taking a pretest. The pretest is available at **www.g-wlearning.com/careereducation/**

LEARNING OUTCOMES

On completion of this chapter, prepare to:

2-1 Identify three common learning styles.

2-2 Recognize resources to identify learning style preferences.

Kinesthetic-tactile learners learn best by touch, by experiences, and by performing hands-on activities.

Elnur/Shutterstock.com

Learning Styles

One of the first steps in developing study skills is to recognize your learning style. Recognizing how you learn can help you define and strengthen how you retain and recall information. People learn in different ways, and there is no one single way to learn. Instead, each person has a unique learning style.

Learning styles are the methods individuals prefer and find most effective for processing and absorbing information. Common learning style preferences are visual, auditory, and kinesthetic-tactile learning, as shown in Figure 2-1.

- **Visual learners** learn best by seeing information or observing things.
- **Auditory learners** learn best by listening to information.
- **Kinesthetic-tactile learners** learn best by performing hands-on or physical activities.

Most people learn in all three ways. One style, however, is often dominant. Before you can develop effective study skills, you must first understand *how* you learn.

Visual Learners

Visual learners *see* to understand. They "learn by seeing," in that, once they can see something, they understand it. For example, when presented with a spoken math problem, a visual learner often responds by saying, "Wait a minute; let me write it down." Seeing the problem on paper is a key to comprehending and processing it. Written language, pictures, charts, and diagrams are most useful to people who prefer this style of learning. Visual learners are described in Figure 2-2.

Visual learners generally prefer to study using pictures, charts, or diagrams and make an effort to visualize things as they learn them. For these learners, visualization is a form of productive daydreaming in which they create images in their

Figure 2-1 There are three common learning style preferences.

Common Learning Style Preferences

Visual learn by seeing

Auditory learn by hearing

Kinesthetic-Tactile learn by touching

Goodheart-Willcox Publisher

Figure 2-2 Visual leaners *see* to understand information.

Visual Learners

- See to learn
- Enjoy quiet reading or study time
- Good at spelling
- Attracted to colors and clear visuals
- Creative
- Careers might relate to graphic designing, photography, architecture, engineering, or computer programming

Goodheart-Willcox Publisher

minds in efforts to see the information. For example, if they are learning about the *Apollo 11* moon landing, they might visualize themselves on the moon, watching as Neil Armstrong and Buzz Aldrin bounce around on the lunar surface.

If information has a tendency to "jump out" of a text and stick in your memory, you are probably a visual learner. If you are a visual learner, the following recommendations will be helpful to improve your study skills.

- When in class, sit where you can see the instructor and any visuals that he or she is using.
- Take notes during lectures.
- Use highlighters to note information to remember.
- Use graphic organizers to help learn concepts.
- Visualize the subject you are studying.
- Use pictures, charts, or diagrams to help you understand the content.

Auditory Learners

Auditory learners *hear* to understand. They learn best when they hear information. Although lecturing is generally considered the least effective teaching method, auditory learners get the most from lectures and often say to the lecturer, "Can you explain that to me?" They prefer to listen to someone talk and share information, rather than read it for themselves. When required to read, they will probably read aloud. Auditory learners are described in Figure 2-3.

Figure 2-3 Auditory learners *hear* to understand information.

Auditory Learners

- Hear to learn
- Enjoy music or audio recordings
- Good at explaining information
- Like to talk
- Prefers spoken directions
- Careers might relate to interpreters/translators, law/politics, journalism, music, or counseling

Goodheart-Willcox Publisher

Auditory learners often remember what others say very well and prefer to discuss ideas they do not immediately understand. Speaking is easy for them, and their vocabularies are usually well developed. They are not afraid to speak in class and are good in study groups.

If you are the type of student who can merely show up to class and actively listen to a topic and is able to pass the exam, you are likely an auditory learner. If you are an auditory learner, the following recommendations will be helpful to improve your study skills.

- When in class, sit where you can hear the instructor.

- Read your assignments aloud.

- Record lectures (with permission of your instructor) so you can listen to them after class.

- If available, listen to audiobooks.

- Ask questions when something is not clear.

- Talk about ideas and concepts with a friend, classmate, or to yourself.

Kinesthetic-Tactile Learners

Kinesthetic-tactile learners *touch* to learn. **Kinesthetic** refers to bodily movement. **Tactile** refers to the sense of touch. People who prefer this learning style usually enjoy touching, discovery, and action. Some of the behaviors of this learner are listed in Figure 2-4.

These people learn best by doing or through hands-on activity. They often say, "Let me play around with it for a while." They use their hands when they talk and learn skills through imitation and practice. These learners are usually good at activities requiring dexterity and hands-on experience such as drawing, cooking, and construction.

Sitting through a lecture might be difficult for these learners because they prefer to be out moving and learning something. A kinesthetic-tactile learner might discover that he or she can concentrate and study most effectively while moving around. Reading while walking on a treadmill, for example, might be a good choice for this type of learner.

If you learn best by performing hands-on applications of the information presented in a lesson, you are likely a kinesthetic-tactile learner. If you are a

Figure 2-4 Kinesthetic-tactile learners *touch* to learn information.

Kinesthetic-Tactile Learners

- Learn through experiences and doing things
- Energetic
- Enjoy experimenting
- Like to move
- Like to work with their hands
- Careers might relate to dancing, sports, construction, physical and occupational therapy, mechanics, or anything physical

Goodheart-Willcox Publisher

kinesthetic-tactile learner, the following recommendations will be helpful to improve your study skills.

- When in class, sit where you will not disturb others if you feel the need to move around.
- Take frequent study breaks.
- Break study time into short periods rather than one long one.
- Rather than study at a desk, walk around.
- Find opportunities for hands-on learning such as building models to represent a lesson.
- Study with others.

Identify Your Learning Style

After reading the descriptions on learning styles, can you identify your learning style preference? Think about your interests or characteristics. Do you enjoy working with visuals? Are you a strong listener? Are you always on the move? There are multiple resources that can help in your self-assessment including

- an instructor;
- free online self-assessment tools;
- a guidance counselor; and
- friends or members from your study group.

You may find that your learning style preference changes based on a task or at different points in your life. The changes can be the result of maturity or experience gained from school or work. There may even be times when you find yourself applying a combination of learning styles. Self-assessment can help you discover more about who you are as a person and influence your learning style preference as you mature as an individual.

An instructor can be a good resource for guidance when learning about personal learning style preferences.

Monkey Business Images/Shutterstock.com

SUMMARY

- **(LO 2-1) Identify three common learning styles.**
  A visual learner learns best by seeing information or observing things. An auditory learner learns best by listening to information. A kinesthetic-tactile learner learns best by performing hands-on or physical activities.
- **(LO 2-2) Recognize resources to identify learning style preferences.**
  There are multiple resources that can help you identify your learning style including an instructor, free online self-assessment tools, a guidance counselor, friends, or members of a study group.

GLOSSARY TERMS

Visit the G-W Learning companion website at **www.g-wlearning.com/careereducation/** to review the following glossary terms.

learning style	kinesthetic-tactile learner
visual learner	kinesthetic
auditory learner	tactile

REVIEW

1. Why is understanding how you learn helpful in developing study skills?

2. Identify three common learning styles.

3. Briefly describe visual learners.

4. What are some study skills that can be useful for visual learners?

5. List examples of characteristics of auditory learners.

6. Define the difference between *kinesthetic* and *tactile*.

7. Why may sitting in a lecture hall be challenging for a kinesthetic-tactile learner?

8. Name two ways in which a kinesthetic-tactile learner can learn more effectively.

9. List resources to use to help identify your learning style preference.

10. What may cause a learning style preference to change?

CRITICAL THINKING

1. Would you describe your learning style preference as visual, auditory, or kinesthetic-tactile? What characteristics do you exhibit that support your identification of your learning style?

2. How can you maximize your personal learning style preference to develop good study skills?

3. Why is it important for you to understand your learning style preference?

4. Explain how you might be able to help a classmate find a study strategy that works for him or her. What kinds of questions would you ask before making suggestions?

5. Do you think it is possible to change from one type of learner into another type over time? Explain why or why not.

INTERNET ACTIVITY

Learning Style Preferences Assessment. Understanding your personal learning style can help you become a better student. Conduct an Internet search for a *learning style assessment*. After you have completed the assessment, compare the results with what you already know about yourself. Were there any surprises?

SKILLS PRACTICE

Visit the G-W Learning companion website at **www.g-wlearning.com/careereducation/** to access and complete the following study skills practice activity:

Study Skills Activity 2-1 Learning Style Scenarios. Each student has his or her own learning style and method of studying. Open the 2-1 file and read each scenario. Using the information you learned in the chapter, recommend study skills for each student based on his or her learning style.

CHAPTER 3

Developing Time-Management Skills

Brian A Jackson/Shutterstock.com

BEFORE YOU READ

Before you begin reading this chapter, see what you already know about time management by taking a pretest. The pretest is available at **www.g-wlearning.com/careereducation/**

LEARNING OUTCOMES

On completion of this chapter, prepare to:

3-1 Describe time management.

3-2 State the elements of a SMART goal.

3-3 Explain why an individual should be flexible when managing his or her time.

Syda Productions/Shutterstock.com

Without time management, one or more activities or tasks will probably not be accomplished when it needs to be.

Time-Management Strategies

An important component of study skills is learning to manage your time. **Time management** is the practice of organizing time and work assignments to increase personal efficiency. It is necessary because your days as a student are filled with academic priorities as well as potential job responsibilities, sports teams, and social commitments. There will be days when you must decide which activities are most important as well as have tasks that must be completed. Without time management, one or more activities or tasks will probably not be accomplished when they need to be.

There are many techniques that can be used to manage your time as illustrated in Figure 3-1. Examples of these strategies are to use a calendar or planner, learn to prioritize, and evaluate personal progress.

Use a Calendar or Planner

Time management requires discipline and starts with creating a schedule or calendar of commitments that you are obligated to meet. Some people opt to use a calendar or spreadsheet on their digital devices to record appointments, tasks, and other obligations. Others prefer to keep a printed schedule or calendar. Inexpensive calendars or planners can be purchased at an office supply store or online. Alternatively, you can download a calendar from the Internet as shown in Figure 3-2.

If selecting a printed version, choose a daily appointment calendar with the date, day of the week, and time slots preprinted. Also, look for one with additional space where you can record tasks that need to be completed and other notes. Figure 3-3 shows the bottom portion of a calendar with space for a to-do list.

Start your time-management routine by filling in your calendar with your class schedule. Most importantly, your school assignments should be a top priority. Read the course syllabus for each class you are taking and schedule your school assignments. Record what they are and when they are due. Include notations about when you need to start lengthy assignments. If you have a paper that must be submitted, you will need multiple days to write it. Avoid waiting until the last minute to study or complete an assignment.

For each appointment or meeting you have, record the day it will take place, who it is with, where you must meet the person, and a contact name and number so you can call the person in the event you need to cancel or reschedule the appointment. If you have a part-time job, record your work hours on your calendar each week. For sports or other commitments, record pertinent information so you can plan your days around them.

When creating your schedule, remember to schedule free time. If you do not schedule an hour or so for yourself each day, you probably will not have it. Having planned free time for yourself ensures productivity and helps to avoid burnout.

Figure 3-1 Time management is the practice of organizing time and work assignments to increase personal efficiency.

Techniques for Time Management

Maintain a calendar › Create a to-do list › Prioritize tasks › Set goals › Schedule free time › Evaluate progress › Be flexible

Goodheart-Willcox Publisher

Figure 3-2 A calendar or planner should have time slots preprinted so information can be easily inserted.

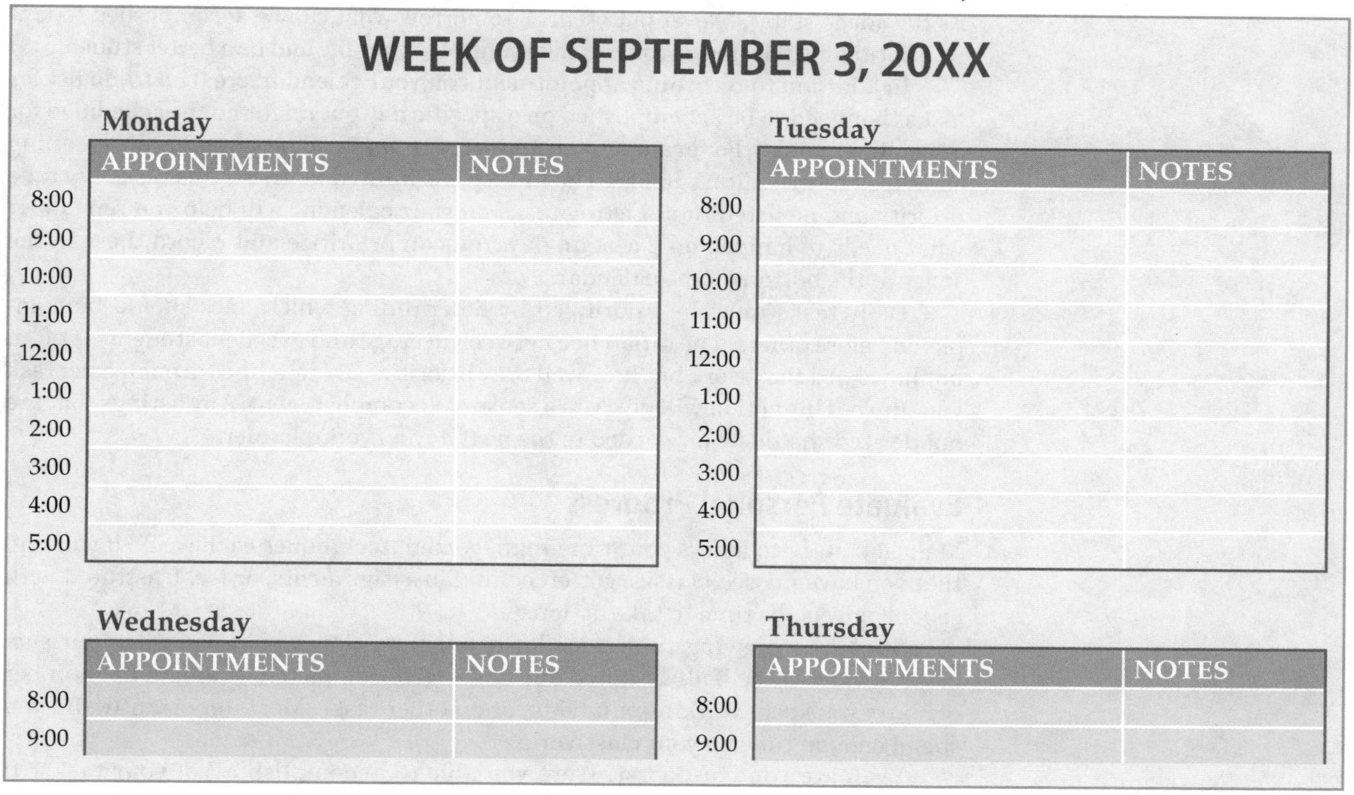

WEEK OF SEPTEMBER 3, 20XX

Monday

APPOINTMENTS	NOTES
8:00	
9:00	
10:00	
11:00	
12:00	
1:00	
2:00	
3:00	
4:00	
5:00	

Tuesday

APPOINTMENTS	NOTES
8:00	
9:00	
10:00	
11:00	
12:00	
1:00	
2:00	
3:00	
4:00	
5:00	

Wednesday

APPOINTMENTS	NOTES
8:00	
9:00	

Thursday

APPOINTMENTS	NOTES
8:00	
9:00	

Goodheart-Willcox Publisher

Figure 3-3 When selecting a printed calendar or planner to use, look for one with space for writing notes or lists.

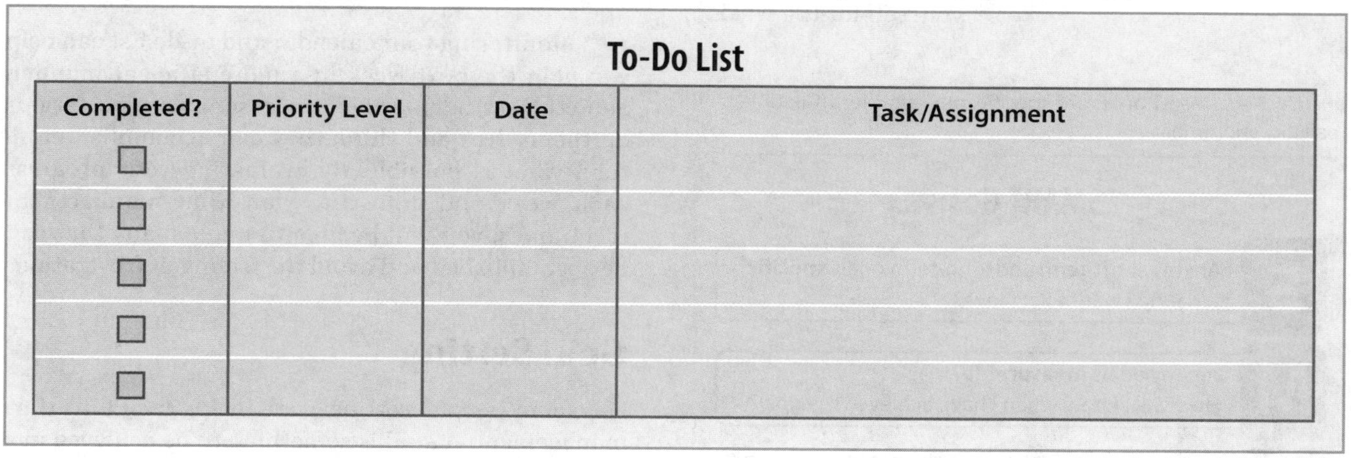

To-Do List

Completed?	Priority Level	Date	Task/Assignment
☐			
☐			
☐			
☐			
☐			

Goodheart-Willcox Publisher

A good habit to establish is to use the weekend to update your calendar for the coming week. Then, begin each morning by reviewing your calendar for appointments and tasks for that day. This will help you feel organized before you leave for school or work.

Prioritize

To **prioritize** means to determine the order of importance in which tasks should be completed. Prioritizing can help you avoid procrastination. **Procrastination** means putting off a task until a later time. Everyone procrastinates at some point in the course of a day or week. This usually results, however, in tasks never actually being completed. As the adage states, "Never put off until tomorrow what can be accomplished today." By prioritizing daily tasks, you can take control of your life and be a better student.

In addition to recording appointments on your calendar, create a to-do list for tasks that need to be accomplished on a specific day but might not be scheduled for a specific time slot. For example, you may need to stop and pick up your dry cleaning as well as return library books. The library has limited hours so this task may take priority and be listed first. Listing tasks on your calendar will help you remember what needs to happen on a certain day. You can prioritize and record these in the space at the bottom of the calendar.

Daily tasks must be prioritized by determining which ones should be completed before others. The difference between average and excellent students is often not how hard they work but how well they prioritize. Draw a line through each task you finish. This action will give you a sense of accomplishment. Any listings that are not deleted should be forwarded to the next day on your planner.

Evaluate Personal Progress

Make it a point to assess your time-management techniques each week. If you find that you have missed classes, gotten behind in assignments, or feel frustrated with school, now is the time to take action.

Start by reviewing your calendar or planner. How would you rate your success? Review to see if all assigned due dates were completed. Evaluate the number of hours you spent working, studying, or on other tasks. Most importantly, did you spend enough time on your classwork?

Evaluate your to-do list. Were you able to accomplish all of your tasks? If they were not all crossed off as completed, stop and reflect on the ones that you did not accomplish and what got in your way of taking care of them. It could have been an unexpected event, or you may simply have expected too much of yourself for the week.

Monitoring your calendar and to-do list can help you plan the next week in a more efficient manner. Sometimes students place unreasonable expectations on themselves and think they can accomplish more than what is possible. By evaluating your progress each week and adjusting your time-management techniques, you will be able to make plans that can be accomplished and avoid the feeling of frustration.

Goal Setting

For some people, setting goals helps facilitate time management. A **goal** is something to be achieved in a specified time period. **Goal setting** is the process of deciding what needs to be achieved and defining the period of time in which to achieve it. There are two types of goals: short-term and long-term. A *short-term goal* is one that can be achieved in less than one year. A *long-term goal* is one that will take a longer period of time to achieve, usually more than one year.

Well-defined goals, including career goals, follow the SMART goal model. **SMART goals** are goals that are specific, measurable, attainable, realistic, and timely as shown in Figure 3-4.

Figure 3-4 SMART goals are specific, measurable, attainable, realistic, and timely.

Goodheart-Willcox Publisher

Specific

A goal should be specific and straightforward. For example, "I want to major in education" is not specific. Instead, you might say, "I want to be a high school science teacher." When the goal is specific, it is easier to track your progress. It also helps in identifying tasks that need to be completed in order to achieve the goal.

Measurable

It is important to be able to measure progress so you know when you have reached your goal. For example, "I want to earn a 90 percent on the biology test" is a measurable goal. When you earn the grade, you will know your goal has been reached.

Attainable

Goals need to be attainable. For example, "I want to be a school principal within two years of graduating" is not a reasonable goal at the starting point of a person's career. Gaining work experience is necessary before obtaining an executive position. The goal of being principal becomes more attainable when coupled with a plan to gain the necessary skills and experience.

Realistic

Goals must be realistic. Attainability and realism are often confused. Having an attainable goal means you have the skills to achieve it. A realistic goal, on the other hand, means the goal fits into your current situation. For example, you might have a goal to run a marathon. This goal is certainly attainable, but if you have not been training for a marathon, the goal is unrealistic. Comparatively, obtaining a position as a principal might be attainable with proper planning and experience. It is much more realistic, however, for an entry-level employee to find work as a teacher first.

Timely

A goal should have starting and ending points. Setting a timeframe to achieve a goal is a step often overlooked. An end date can help you stay on track. For example, you might want to be a principal by the time you are 40 years old. Aiming to get the experience and education to achieve this position by a specific age will help you remain motivated to reach your goal on time.

Being Flexible

Managing your time will bring you great rewards in your personal and academic life. Once you establish a routine of creating schedules, you might find that you actually like them. You will enjoy the sense of accomplishment that comes with checking off things on your to-do list and meeting your goals. When you have free time to yourself, you will know time management paid off.

Above all, be flexible in managing your time. No one is a perfect manager of time. Unplanned events happen—you get a new job, come down with the flu, or adopt a new pet. Do not be hard on yourself when life happens and you lose control of your management routine for a few days. Take a deep breath, take some time, and then get back to your schedule when it makes sense for you. Remember to reward yourself for your successes. When you have days off for vacation or holidays, put the schedules away.

Monitoring a calendar and to-do list helps plan the next week in a more efficient manner.

Rawpixel.com/Shutterstock.com

SUMMARY

- **(LO 3-1) Describe time management.**
  Time management is the practice of organizing time and work assignments to increase personal efficiency. Three examples of time-management strategies are to use a calendar or planner, learn to prioritize, and evaluate personal progress.
- **(LO 3-2) State the elements of a SMART goal.**
  A goal is something to be achieved in a specific time period. A SMART goal is one that is specific, measurable, attainable, realistic, and timely.
- **(LO 3-3) Explain why an individual should be flexible when managing his or her time.**
  No one is a perfect manager of time. Unplanned events happen and it is important to be flexible.

GLOSSARY TERMS

Visit the G-W Learning companion website at **www.g-wlearning.com/careereducation/** to review the following glossary terms.

time management	goal
prioritize	goal setting
procrastination	SMART goal

REVIEW

1. Discuss time management.

2. List examples of three strategies to use for time management.

3. Discuss the different options available when selecting a calendar or planner.

4. Identify steps to take when completing a calendar for the coming week.

5. Why is it important to create a to-do list of tasks?

6. What are some ways to evaluate progress of your time-management techniques?

7. State the difference between a short-term goal and a long-term goal.

8. What are the elements of a SMART goal?

9. Compare and contrast an attainable goal and a realistic goal.

10. Why should you be flexible with your schedule?

CRITICAL THINKING

1. When it comes to keeping track of assignments and tasks, do you prefer to use a calendar or a planner? Is it print or digital? Explain why the choice works for you.

2. Evaluate your time-management techniques from last week. Recall any assignments you had due, meetings or sports practices, or other activities. How successful was your time management? Why do you think it is important to evaluate your time-management success at the end of the week?

3. Time-management techniques include planning, prioritizing tasks, and evaluating personal progress. Elaborate on how you use these techniques in your time-management routine.

4. Prioritizing tasks is a key to good time management. What is your approach to prioritizing your activities or tasks?

5. Reflect on your ability to manage time. Discuss your strengths and weaknesses. How can you improve your time-management skills?

INTERNET ACTIVITY

Time Management. Personal Information Management (PIM) is a system individuals use to acquire, organize, maintain, retrieve, and use information, such as Microsoft Outlook. Conduct an Internet search for *Personal Information Management (PIM) systems*. Review the different types of systems available and choose one that you believe suits your needs. How can utilizing a PIM system benefit you as a student and in your personal life?

SKILLS PRACTICE

Visit the G-W Learning companion website at **www.g-wlearning.com/careereducation/** to access and complete the following study skills practice activities:

Study Skills Activity 3-1 Calendar. Time management requires discipline and starts with creating a schedule or calendar of commitments that you are obligated to meet. Open the 3-1 file, and create a calendar for next week. Include all appointments, deadlines, and any other commitments you may have. In addition, prioritize your tasks using the to-do list at the bottom of the calendar.

Study Skills Activity 3-2 SMART Goals. Developing SMART goals is an essential element of good study skills. Open the 3-2 file, and write a goal you have for next semester. Evaluate the goal against the criteria for a SMART goal.

Study Skills Activity 3-3 Managing Your Time. Knowing how you spend your time each day can help you understand how to improve your time-management skills. Complete the activity in the 3-3 file to create a circle graph depicting the proportions of time you spend on various activities during a week.

Study Skills Activity 3-4 Time-Management Advice. As you learn how to manage your time, you can help others master this skill as well. Open the 3-4 file and read the situations provided. Write the advice you would give to each person.

Defining Study Time

Yunus Malik/Shutterstock.com

BEFORE YOU READ

Before you begin reading this chapter, see what you already know about study time by taking a pretest. The pretest is available at **www.g-wlearning.com/careereducation/**

LEARNING OUTCOMES

On completion of this chapter, prepare to:

4-1 List examples of factors to consider when defining study time.

4-2 Identify examples of study techniques.

4-3 Explain the concept of cramming.

Study time is the block of time designated to complete homework, read materials for class, or work on other assignments that must be accomplished according to a specific schedule.

Phovoir/Shutterstock.com

Define Your Study Time

Study time is the block of minutes or hours designated to complete homework, read materials for class, or work on other assignments that must be accomplished according to a specific time schedule. Without a designated study time schedule, it can be challenging to pass a class.

As you learned in the previous chapter, study time should be the first priority in your time-management routine. Assigning regular blocks of time on your calendar or planner will ensure adequate time to complete class work. Your school assignments are top priority.

There are many factors involved when defining a study session. Some factors include the number of classes in which you are enrolled, length of the material you plan to study, and time of day during which you will be studying.

Class Load

If you are a college student, your instructors will probably tell you to spend a minimum of two hours of study time for each credit hour class that you are taking. A typical class is usually three credit hours. This means you should study at least six hours per week for each class. If you are taking four classes, that adds up to a total of 24 hours of study time each week, give or take a few hours.

On your calendar, you should record each class that you attend and separate entries to designate times you will spend studying. If you are taking 12 hours of classes and studying 24 hours, that is a total of 36 hours per week of school commitments. Going to school is a full-time job! Time management will be very important to make sure your schoolwork is a priority over other activities in which you are involved.

Length of Study Time

The length of each study session depends largely on the task at hand. If there is a great deal to be studied, an optimal study period is two hours for any one sitting. Keep in mind that multiple short study sessions can be more effective than a single long one. For some students, breaking the time into 30- to 60-minute sessions is more effective than studying for two straight hours.

An important, yet often overlooked, factor in studying is scheduling breaks. During a potentially lengthy study session, you might experience a **burnout**, which is a loss of interest due to an overload of work or information. To help avoid burnouts, it is suggested that you schedule breaks in between your study sessions. A good rule to follow is take a 5–10 minute break in between one-hour study sessions. Studying in shorter but repetitive sessions helps reduce eyestrain, avoids burnouts, and maintains your interest in the material.

Your learning style and personality play significant roles in determining how long to study at one time. For example, kinesthetic-tactile learners might find they need to take longer or more frequent breaks while reviewing class notes. Visual learners, however, might be able to go longer periods of time reading or reviewing notes without a break.

Time of Day

The time of day at which you study is a personal preference. It is likely that you feel most alert at a certain time of day. Some people are morning people, others concentrate best during the midday hours, and still others are "night owls," who are most productive in the evening.

Studies have shown that morning is a better time to review test materials, write reports, and complete analytical work, such as mathematics and problem-solving activities. Midday is best for activities involving movement, such as clerical work and practicing artistic abilities. The afternoon is the best time for reading and a good time to study literature and history courses.

Most people are more alert during daylight hours. An added advantage of daytime studying is that libraries are open if you require them. In addition, getting in touch with fellow students for help is probably easier during the day than if you are studying late at night.

Many students prefer to study in the evening and stay up all night, when necessary, preparing for class the next day. Some students are forced to study at night because of busy class and work schedules. Advantages of nighttime studying are that it is probably quiet and there are fewer interruptions. One disadvantage is that many people are tired, and studying can be a struggle. If nighttime studying is your choice, make sure you are well rested before you begin.

Study Techniques

Selecting a study technique that works for you is just as important as the studying space you use. As you progress through school, you will learn which techniques work for you. You will find that you can improve some techniques to better suit you, and you might discover some ineffective techniques you should abandon. Some common study techniques that many people find useful include prioritizing the subjects to be studied, forming a study group, or taking practice tests. Additional techniques are noted in Figure 4-1.

Prioritize Subjects

If you have multiple classes for which to study, prioritize the subjects. To prioritize means to rank items in order from most to least important. Prioritizing is a technique that helps you manage and organize your work.

One way to prioritize is to give your attention first to the hardest subject or the one you think is most boring. Getting this completed first helps rid you of anxiety. If you are dreading an assignment, it is better to complete it first rather than be distracted from your other studies by thinking about how you are going to get it finished. In addition, the dreaded subjects might take more time than you originally planned. By tackling them first, you might realize that you need to adjust or extend your study time to accomplish everything on your list.

Figure 4-1 Study techniques are equally as important as a study space and can be adapted to fit an individual's needs.

Study Techniques

- adapt methods that fit learning style
- apply time-management skills
- avoid multitasking
- create flash cards
- create study environment
- focus on materials
- prioritize subjects
- review class notes
- take practice tests
- turn off digital devices
- use mnemonics for memorization
- utilize study groups

Goodheart-Willcox Publisher

Group Study

Forming a study group to prepare for a presentation or an exam is a technique that can be beneficial to you and other group members. Studying with others who have a similar learning style as you have might help reinforce what you are studying, and you and the others can help each other. By contrast, studying with people who have different learning styles from you might help you learn and remember things in a different way. There are many advantages of a study group, in that notes can be shared, subject matter can be discussed, and other input can be made for preparing for a class or test.

Practice Testing

Practice testing is the strategy of taking advantage of self-assessment opportunities. Practice testing is a great opportunity to learn without the fear of a grade.

A good place to begin is to read the objectives at the beginning of the chapter. Turn each objective into a question then try to answer it. Objectives are generally the basis for test questions. If you can answer each question you create, you should understand the basic content in the chapter.

Next, review the end-of-chapter questions, practice tests, or lab manuals that accompany a textbook. These provide excellent opportunities to practice or self-assess what you have learned. Take the time to answer questions or work through an exercise without using the text or class notes. Then, using the text or notes, confirm your responses. By evaluating how many questions are correct, you can identify the material in which you are confident while noting content that may need additional review. Chances are good that if you complete all the activities accompanying a chapter in a text, you will probably do well on an exam.

Cramming should be avoided as it involves trying to memorize a large amount of information in a short amount of time.

Cramming

Cramming is the practice of studying intensely to absorb a large volume of information in a short period of time. This is often done at the last minute as students enter the classroom or immediately prior to a test. It is usually the result of poor time management.

Cramming is *not* a desirable technique to use. Most educators discourage it because it often results in a lack of long-term retention of the material. As such, cramming should generally be avoided. As a last resort, however, it can be effective for an impending test. If cramming is necessary, focus on chapter summaries or key points, which typically appear in the end-of-chapter material.

SUMMARY

- **(LO 4-1) List examples of factors to consider when defining study time.**
  Examples of factors to consider when defining study time include the number of classes you are enrolled in, length of the material you plan to study, and time of day during which you will be studying.
- **(LO 4-2) Identify examples of study techniques.**
  Some common study techniques that many people find useful include prioritizing the subjects to be studied, forming a study group, and taking practice tests.
- **(LO 4-3) Explain the concept of cramming.**
  Cramming is the practice of studying intensely to absorb a large volume of information in a short period of time. This is often done at the last minute as students enter the classroom or immediately prior to a test and is often the result of poor time management. Cramming is *not* a desirable technique to use and should generally be avoided. As a last resort, however, it can be effective for an impending test.

GLOSSARY TERMS

Visit the G-W Learning companion website at **www.g-wlearning.com/careereducation/** to review the following glossary terms.

study time   cramming
burnout

REVIEW

1. Identify factors to consider when defining your study time.

2. How many hours of study time should you plan for each credit hour of class per week?

3. Why is studying in short but repetitive sessions necessary for effective studying?

4. State a benefit of studying during daylight hours and a benefit for studying during nighttime hours.

5. List three examples of effective study techniques.

6. Why is it a good study technique to complete the hardest subject first?

7. Name two advantages of participating in a study group.

8. What is practice testing?

9. Why is cramming *not* usually recommended as a study technique?

10. If cramming is necessary as a last resort, on what content should you focus?

CRITICAL THINKING

1. Optimal length of study time can vary depending on factors such as an individual's personal needs, learning style preference, and types of assignments. Explain the strategies you use to determine the number of hours you spend studying per subject. Discuss the effectiveness of the strategies you use.

2. Do you prefer to study during the morning, midday, afternoon, or evening? How does time of day influence your ability to study?

3. Describe the study techniques that work best for you. Why are these techniques effective?

4. Review the assignments or tasks you will have next week. Identify the materials you need to read for class and the assignments that must be accomplished according to a specific time schedule. Describe how you will prioritize the assignments. List them in order and the amount of time needed to complete each one.

5. Recall a time when you did not adequately study for a test or prepare for an assignment. Did you end up cramming at the last minute? What were the results? What will you do differently in the future to avoid cramming?

INTERNET ACTIVITY

Study Group. Study groups can be an effective way to get to know classmates, as well as share information and be better prepared for class. Conduct an Internet search for *how to create a study group*. Summarize the steps to creating a study group that can be effective for all its members.

Cramming. Cramming is not a desirable study technique to use. There might be a time, however, when cramming is a last resort to prepare for an exam. Conduct an Internet search on *how to cram successfully*. Summarize what you learn.

SKILLS PRACTICE

Visit the G-W Learning companion website at **www.g-wlearning.com/careereducation/** to access and complete the following study skills practice activity:

Study Skills Activity 4-1 Class Load. The number of classes in which you are enrolled affects how much study time you need. Open the 4-1 file, and list each class you are taking and the credit hours for each class. Based on the number of classes and credit hours, estimate how much time you should be spending each week studying.

CHAPTER 5

Creating a Study Environment

Good Mood/Shutterstock.com

BEFORE YOU READ

Before you begin reading this chapter, see what you already know about study environments by taking a pretest. The pretest is available at **www.g-wlearning.com/careereducation/**

LEARNING OUTCOMES

On completion of this chapter, prepare to:

5-1 List considerations to be made when planning an effective study space.

5-2 Identify examples of distractions to avoid when studying.

Creating Your Study Environment

A **study environment** is the place where you read your textbooks, review your school materials, complete your assignments, and prepare for tests. It can be your bedroom, the library, or the kitchen in the place where you live. A study environment is any specific location where you are comfortable and confident that you can successfully complete work assigned to you.

The type of study environment you choose is a personal decision. Keep in mind that the ideal environment for you might be very different from the ideal environment for a friend. Considerations should be made for space, supplies, lighting, temperature, and proper ergonomics.

A study environment is a place where textbooks are read, school materials reviewed, assignments completed, and test preparation takes place.

wavebreakmedia/Shutterstock.com

Space

An important consideration for an effective study area is to find a clean and organized place. If you study at the kitchen table and there are dirty dishes in front of you, you will lose your focus. In addition, spilled food or drinks can ruin your papers and other materials. If your bedroom is your study environment, a desk piled with clothing or books will be a distraction.

Establishing a permanent place to study is an optimal situation. A permanent study place will probably be your bedroom or dorm room but could be any space that you find comfortable. Knowing that your space is there, organized, and ready to use eliminates preparation time and deciding where to study. If you have the luxury of creating a personal and permanent location, take advantage of the opportunity.

Supplies

Before you sit down and begin studying, take time to clean up and organize your study area. You will lose time if you have to stop and find a book or other materials you need. Make sure you have paper, pens, highlighters, or any other office supplies you think might be required to complete an assignment. Collect all your references and notes and place them where they can be accessed easily. If a computer is necessary, make sure there is an outlet close by in the event that the battery needs to be recharged.

Lighting

The lighting in a study environment can make a difference in your success. A well-lit environment can increase your alertness and positively influence your attitude. Poor lighting, including harsh, artificial lighting, can lead to eyestrain, headaches, and fatigue.

Natural light is ideal if it is available. During daylight hours, try sitting near a source of natural light such as a window or door. If studying at night, use a desk lamp and position it to shine light directly on your book or papers. Place the lamp on the side opposite of your writing hand to avoid shadows on your work area.

Temperature

Decide if you prefer to study in a cool or warm environment. Studies have shown that the temperature of a study area can play an important role in student scores and memory ability. Students working in temperatures that are too high (over 80 degrees Fahrenheit) or too low (under 70 degrees Fahrenheit) tend to have lower test scores than those working in moderate temperatures (70–75 degrees Fahrenheit). Try to find a place in which you are comfortable. Dressing in layers is a good method for adjusting to your environment's temperature.

Ergonomics

An ergonomic workspace should be found in which to study. **Ergonomics** is the science of adapting a workstation to fit the needs of a person. Applying ergonomic principles results in a comfortable and efficient environment.

Comfortable, ergonomic furniture is needed for an effective study area. Some people find that they prefer a formal posture when studying, which might mean sitting in a comfortable chair and reading or writing at a table or desk. Your chair should allow your knees to be even with or slightly below your hips, and your feet should rest flat on the floor.

If you are using a computer monitor, the screen should be approximately an arm's length away from your face, and the top of the screen should be near eye level. When keying, your elbow should be bent at a 90-degree angle or greater. Finding a setup that fits your unique needs will provide the most efficient and safest study environment for you. Figure 5-1 identifies a comfortable ergonomic workstation.

Figure 5-1 An ergonomic workstation helps prevent back and neck pain, eyestrain, and headaches.

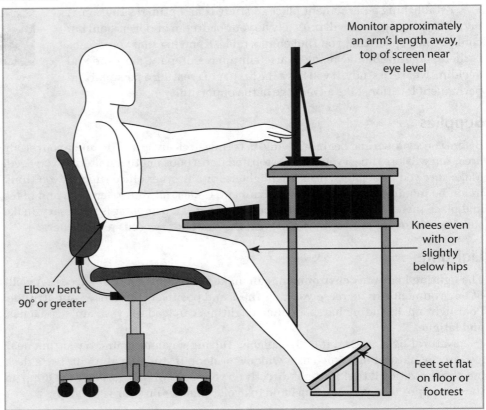

Goodheart-Willcox Publisher

Be aware of the dangers of eyestrain, and take precautions to avoid it. When spending a lot of time in front of a computer, tablet, or smartphone screen, you should take frequent breaks to rest your eyes. Enlarging the font size might help alleviate excess strain on your eyes. Dimming the screen light and using antiglare or antireflective screens are also good options to keep your eyes healthy.

Avoiding Distractions

A study environment should be free from distractions. Each time someone or something takes your attention away from studying, you lose time and concentration. Distractions can come in many forms including friends, music, and digital devices.

A "Do Not Disturb" sign can discourage friends from stopping by to chat while studying is in progress.

Friends

Unless friends are studying with you, their appearance can cause a distraction. If you think there is a chance friends might see you and stop by, let them know in advance that you are studying and do not wish to be bothered. A study environment with a door is a luxury. If you are lucky enough to have a door, close it when your study session begins. Consider hanging a "Do Not Disturb" sign on the doorknob to discourage friends from stopping by to chat.

Anikei/Shutterstock.com

Music

Many people need to study in an environment with no noise. Others, however, do not require a perfectly quiet environment and might even prefer some background music. In fact, research has shown that background music can be a study aid. As long as the music is not too loud or distracting, it might help drown out other sounds and might even help you remember what you are studying.

While research has shown that background music can be a study aid, studying while wearing headphones tends to lower memory and information retention. If music helps you study, consider listening to a radio at a low volume instead of using headphones with a portable device.

Digital Devices

Digital devices that are unessential to studying should not be present in your study environment. If you require a computer as a tool to study, consider deactivating the Wi-Fi or disconnecting the Internet cable if the Internet is not essential for your studies. In addition, turn off your phone so your incoming calls, messages, or notifications do not distract you.

SUMMARY

- **(LO 5-1) List considerations to be made when planning an effective study space.**
  Considerations for an effective study space should be made for space, supplies, lighting, temperature, and proper ergonomics.
- **(LO 5-2) Identify examples of distractions to avoid when studying.**
  Distractions can come in many forms including friends, music, and digital devices.

GLOSSARY TERMS

Visit the G-W Learning companion website at **www.g-wlearning.com/careereducation/** to review the following glossary terms.

study environment   ergonomics

REVIEW

1. What is a study environment?

2. Identify factors that should be considered when creating a study space.

3. State an advantage of establishing a permanent place to study.

4. What are examples of benefits of a well-lit study environment?

5. What is the effect of studying in temperatures that are too high or too low?

6. Identify elements of an ergonomic study area.

7. List examples of external distractions that can interrupt study time.

8. How can you minimize distractions caused by friends?

9. Why should you not wear headphones while studying?

10. If a computer is required for studying, what can you do to limit distractions caused by the device?

CRITICAL THINKING

1. Describe your current study environment.

2. List ways in which you can improve your current study environment.

3. Describe an ideal ergonomic workstation that would work for you.

4. List distractions that typically keep you from focusing on your assignments at hand. How can you eliminate those distractions in the future?

5. Describe an environment in which you have previously tried to study that was inappropriate for one reason or another. How did this affect your study session?

INTERNET ACTIVITY

Study Environment. The ideal study environment for one person might be vastly different from the ideal study environment for another person. Conduct an Internet search for *conducive study environment*. How would you compare your study environment to the results of your research?

SKILLS PRACTICE

Visit the G-W Learning companion website at **www.g-wlearning.com/careereducation/** to access and complete the following study skills practice activity:

Study Skills Activity 5-1 My Study Environment. Identify your favorite place to study. Open the 5-1 file. Complete the graphic organizer by describing the elements of your study environment. Include where your study environment is located and the items that you utilize.

CHAPTER 6

Improving Reading Comprehension

Steve Cukrov/Shutterstock.com

BEFORE YOU READ

Before you begin reading this chapter, see what you already know about reading comprehension by taking a pretest. The pretest is available at **www.g-wlearning.com/careereducation/**

LEARNING OUTCOMES

On completion of this chapter, prepare to:

6-1 Explain reading comprehension.

6-2 List ways to improve vocabulary.

6-3 Identify examples of routines to establish when learning new words.

Supplement materials that you are assigned in class with reading selections of your own.

Dean Drobot/Shutterstock.com

Reading Comprehension

As a student, you have the responsibility to read textbooks, materials your instructor assigns, and supplemental materials that help you learn the subject matter of the class in which you are enrolled. It is also necessary that you comprehend what you read. To **comprehend** means to grasp, or understand. **Reading comprehension** is the ability to understand what has been read. It involves processing the words and decoding their meaning so that the reader can grasp what is being conveyed.

Understanding how words are formed can help your reading comprehension. In addition, learning how to derive meaning from context clues can help you comprehend the content that is being conveyed.

Etymology

Increasing the number of recognizable words to help with comprehension begins with becoming familiar with etymology. **Etymology** is the origin of a word and the historical development of its meaning. Etymology consists of studying types of word parts: affixes, primarily prefixes and suffixes, and root words, as shown in Figure 6-1. Studying word parts can help you understand the meaning of a new word.

- A *prefix* is a word or word part added to the beginning of an existing word to create a new meaning.

- A *suffix* is a word or word part added to the end of an existing word to create a new meaning.

- A *root word* is the most basic part of a word and has no prefix or suffix.

Most words can be traced to Latin, Greek, or Indo-European roots. For example, the root word *pac* comes from the Latin word *pax*, meaning "peace." If you are unfamiliar with the meaning of the word *pacify*, but you know *pac* comes from the Latin word for peace, you might be able to deduce that the word *pacify* likely means

Figure 6-1 Studying prefixes, suffixes, and root words can help with understanding the meaning of new words.

Etymology					
Prefixes		**Suffixes**		**Root Words**	
Word	**Meaning**	**Word**	**Meaning**	**Word**	**Meaning**
anti-	against	-able	can be done	-bio-	life
inter-	between	-ed	past-tense verbs	-dict-	say
pre-	before	-ing	present participle of verb	-geo-	earth
re-	again	-ity	state of	-man(u)-	hand
semi-	half	-less	without	-photo-	light

Goodheart-Willcox Publisher

"to bring peace to something." Familiarizing yourself with common prefixes, suffixes, and root words can help you learn new words at a faster rate.

Context Clues

We learn many words we know simply by reading them and manufacturing possible meanings based on context clues. **Context clues** are hints that help define an unfamiliar word based on the surrounding words in a sentence. They can appear in the same sentence as the word or may follow it in a preceding sentence. There are four common types of context clues that can be used to help comprehend what you are reading.

- *Definition clues* provide an explanation of the unknown word within the sentence or immediately following the sentence.

- *Restatement clues*, also called *synonym clues*, are other words used in the sentence with similar meaning.

- *Contrast clues*, also called *antonym clues*, are surrounding words or a phrase with the opposite meaning. They are often signaled by words such as but, whereas, unlike, and as opposed to.

- *Inference clues* are clues that are not directly described but are implied based on the clues within, before, and after the sentence in which the unknown word is used.

You can use context clues in both reading and listening to generate meanings for unfamiliar words. Read this sentence:

> Given the litany of tasks required to be completed by the end of the day, Josie called her mother to let her know she would be late for their scheduled dinner.

Litany might be an unfamiliar word for you. Based on the context of the sentence, however, you can probably conclude that it means "a large number."

Improve Your Vocabulary

Have you ever read a paragraph and realized you did not understand what you read? Maybe you did not understand the content because there were unfamiliar words used. In order to comprehend what you read, you must understand the vocabulary used in the material. An important component of effective study skills is a well-developed vocabulary.

Vocabulary development is a process people use to increase the number of words with which they are familiar. Individuals who understand how to select words, understand their meanings, and use them appropriately succeed in both school and in their personal lives.

A large vocabulary not only makes reading easier and your writing more precise, but it also makes you a better thinker and listener. Investing time into developing your vocabulary will improve your communication skills, help you interact with classmates, and enable you to explain your own thoughts and ideas in a more effective way. To improve your vocabulary, make a point of looking up words you do not understand. If it is inconvenient to check a dictionary while reading, write down unknown words, and look them up later. Reread the document once you learn the meanings of the words. Work especially hard at understanding words and terms commonly used in your classes. Ways to improve your vocabulary include reading voraciously, downloading a vocabulary app, learning a new word every day, and completing crossword puzzles.

Read, Read, Read

Become a voracious reader. **Voracious** means excessively eager. Find written works reflecting your interests and read as much as possible, focusing on the goal of enhancing your vocabulary. If you are interested in sports, read a sports magazine. If you enjoy music, read a book about a musician.

Reading on your own is a form of self-education. Develop the habit of supplementing the materials you are assigned in class with reading selections of your own. By expanding your knowledge through reading, you will increase your self-confidence and become more comfortable with new challenges.

You likely already know how to find a word in the dictionary, so use this skill when you encounter a new word. Reference texts, such as dictionaries and thesauruses, are valuable resources when it comes to building a vocabulary. Keep a dictionary close to where you normally do your reading. When you come across a word you do not know, first try to develop a meaning for it based on contextual clues, and then find the word in the dictionary.

From there, you can search for the word in a thesaurus to find synonyms. A **synonym** is a word with a similar meaning. This method not only teaches you one new word, but possibly several, depending on how many synonyms are listed in the thesaurus.

Digital devices can be used as a tool to improve vocabulary through an online dictionary, thesaurus, or vocabulary app.

Lucky Business/Shutterstock.com

Download a Vocabulary App

Your smartphone can be an excellent tool for expanding your vocabulary. Downloading a vocabulary app is a convenient way to learn new words. Vocabulary apps offer users the opportunity to learn words through interactive games, digital dictionaries, or building a personal collection of terms. Instead of playing basic games when you have free time, you can build your vocabulary while having fun.

Learn a Word of the Day

One simple method allowing you to learn one new word each day is to subscribe to an online dictionary's "word of the day" e-mail. Subscribers receive an e-mail every day that features a word and its meaning. These e-mails usually also contain examples of the word in writing and might even include the etymology of the word or the word's first known usage. This passive learning technique allows information to be delivered to you without you having to seek it out.

An alternative to this is a "word of the day" calendar. You can purchase a calendar with a new word and its definition on the page each day. These words are generally unusual words you might not encounter in your everyday reading.

Work on Crossword Puzzles

The nature of a crossword puzzle requires the person completing the puzzle to be familiar with a vast number of words. These words come from all parts of speech and include both proper and common nouns. You must be able to identify the correct word being referenced and spell it correctly so as not to affect the spelling of a separate word in the puzzle. Therefore, completing crossword puzzles can help you improve not only your vocabulary skills, but your reasoning, spelling, and word-relational skills as well.

Even if you do not know the answer to a clue, you can still enhance your vocabulary. Looking up answers to unknown clues can potentially teach you synonyms or new words entirely. For example, suppose a crossword puzzle contains the clue "to look at with admiration" and you know, based on the number of boxes, that the word is six letters. You might not know the answer, but consulting a thesaurus for the word *admire* will likely supply you with the six-letter word *revere*, a possible answer.

Develop a Routine

How many words do you think you already know, and how many words would you like to know? There are many ways to improve your vocabulary, but it takes some effort on your part. With dedication and conscious motivation, it is possible to learn thousands of new words. Develop a routine for improving your vocabulary.

- Learn a new word each day. If you learn one new word each day, you will learn over 700 words within two years.

- Keep a vocabulary journal. Record each new word you learn along with its definition and part of speech, such as a noun or verb. Write a sentence using the word. Try to use the word in a conversation, class discussion, or written assignment. This will definitively prove whether you truly understand the appropriate usage of the word.

- Practice new words you learn. Aim to set aside a few minutes, for example 15 minutes, a day to practice developing your vocabulary skills. During this time, you can research new words you came across during the day. In addition, you can review words you are in the process of learning.

- Listen to what others are saying. Note unfamiliar words that are spoken and how they are used in a conversation or lecture. *Listening vocabulary* are words a person should know so he or she can understand what was heard. When you hear a word you do not understand, make a note and look up its meaning.

Just like any other new skill, it is important to revisit and practice your vocabulary. Just because you found the definition of a new word in the dictionary does not mean you truly understand the word. Without review, you might forget the meaning of a word, especially if the word is not one you use regularly, or you might not know how to use it correctly in a sentence. Just as a pianist must practice piano in order to keep playing skills sharp, you need to try to implement new words into your vocabulary if you want to be able to use them regularly. If you do not use your new words, it is likely you will lose them.

SUMMARY

- **(LO 6-1) Explain reading comprehension.**
  Reading comprehension is the ability to understand what has been read. Studying etymology and context clues can help you comprehend what you read.
- **(LO 6-2) List ways to improve vocabulary.**
  Ways to improve your vocabulary include reading voraciously, downloading a vocabulary app, learning a new word every day, and completing crossword puzzles.
- **(LO 6-3) Identify examples of routines to establish when learning new words.**
  Routines to establish when learning new words include learn a new word a day, keep a vocabulary journal, revisit and practice your vocabulary, and listen to what others are saying.

GLOSSARY TERMS

Visit the G-W Learning companion website at **www.g-wlearning.com/careereducation/** to review the following glossary terms.

comprehend

reading comprehension

etymology

context clue

vocabulary development

voracious

synonym

REVIEW

1. Explain reading comprehension.

2. What are two actions that can help your reading comprehension?

3. Identify types of word parts studied in etymology.

4. What are four common types of context clues?

5. Discuss some benefits of building a large vocabulary.

6. List examples of ways to improve your vocabulary.

7. Discuss reading as a form of self-education.

8. Explain how you can learn a word every day.

9. Identify examples of routines to establish when learning new words.

10. Why is it important to revisit and practice your vocabulary?

CRITICAL THINKING

1. Explain how learning to comprehend what you are reading will help improve your grades. Why do you believe reading comprehension is important?

2. Recall a time that you came across a word that you did not understand. How did you figure out the meaning of the word? List and describe the resources or tools you used.

3. Identify ways you personally have found to be effective in improving your vocabulary.

4. Discuss how you can expand your vocabulary through reading, viewing, listening, and discussion with others.

5. How do you view yourself as a reader? Do you challenge yourself as a reader? Describe your reading habits and your ability to comprehend the information.

INTERNET ACTIVITY

Reading Comprehension. Reading comprehension will be a key to your success both personally and in school. Conduct an Internet search on *reading comprehension strategies.* List three strategies that you would be willing to try. Explain why you chose these specific ones.

Vocabulary App. One method to improve your vocabulary is to use a vocabulary app on your digital device. Using the Internet, research *apps for vocabulary development.* Choose one that interests you, download it to your device, and use it. Explain which app you chose and how you plan to use it to improve your vocabulary.

Word of the Day. Spending time on vocabulary development can help you become a better student and a well-rounded individual. Conduct an Internet search for *word of the day.* What website did you use? What is the new word and definition you learned?

SKILLS PRACTICE

Visit the G-W Learning companion website at **www.g-wlearning.com/careereducation/** to access and complete the following study skills practice activities:

Study Skills Activity 6-1 Reading Comprehension. Developing your reading comprehension skills can help you understand the content of the material you read. Open the 6-1 file. Complete the reading activity, and focus on the content. After you have read the passage, key your answers to the reading comprehension questions. Then evaluate your reading skills.

Study Skills Activity 6-2 Using Synonyms. A synonym is a word with a similar meaning to another word. To review your understanding of synonyms, open the 6-2 file. Write a synonym for each word provided.

Study Skills Activity 6-3 Using Antonyms. An antonym is a word that is the opposite of another word. To review your understanding of antonyms, open the 6-3 file. Write an antonym for each word provided.

Study Skills Activity 6-4 Analogies. An analogy is a comparison between two items. To review your understanding of analogies, open the 6-4 file, and complete the activity.

Study Skills Activity 6-5 Identifying Misused Words. You should choose words that suit the situations in which they are used. Open the 6-5 file. Read the passage, highlight the correct words, and rekey the paragraphs using the proper words.

Becoming an Active Reader

Angeles College
3440 Wilshire Blvd., Suite 310
Los Angeles, CA 90010
Tel. (213) 487-2211

wavebreakmedia/Shutterstock.com

BEFORE YOU READ

Before you begin reading this chapter, see what you already know about active reading by taking a pretest. The pretest is available at **www.g-wlearning.com/careereducation/**

LEARNING OUTCOMES

On completion of this chapter, prepare to:

7-1   Describe active reading.

7-2   Explain how skimming, scanning, and reading for detail can help a person become a skillful reader.

7-3   Define SQ3R and the five steps of this strategy.

7-4   Identify examples of general reading techniques.

7-5   Summarize strategies to improve reading skills.

Always have a pen ready when reading to make annotations.

Minerva Studio/Shutterstock.com

Active Reading

Active reading is processing the words, phrases, and sentences encountered while reading. It is a complex task involving concentration and determination to understand and evaluate the reading and its relevance to your needs. Active reading requires the reader to use strategies to understand the material so comprehension is possible. To *comprehend* means to grasp, or understand. If you do not grasp what you read, you will not learn what is presented. In order to be successful in school and your career, you must be able to comprehend material you read. You can *self-monitor*, or personally reflect on, your progress and access your comprehension by taking the following actions.

- Consider the writer's purpose for writing. Is the writer comparing and contrasting information, criticizing an idea, or explaining information? Identifying the purpose helps you absorb the message and understand what is being presented.

- Relate what you read to your prior knowledge. **Prior knowledge** is experience and information a person already possesses.

- Be able to summarize what you have read. Once you are finished reading, mentally summarize, or briefly state, the main points of the material. Writing a one-sentence summary about each paragraph is an effective way to demonstrate that you understood what you read.

- Create a reverse outline. This involves creating an outline by writing the topic of each section and briefly explaining how it advances the overall topic of the reading. If the topics in the outline are clear to you, it is a good indication that you comprehended the material.

If there are unfamiliar words, stop and look them up on the Internet or in a print dictionary. Read a paragraph again if you read it and it does not make sense. Evaluate information both as you read and after you read to ensure understanding. Consider the questions and comments you think about as you read.

Reading Skillfully

Most people take reading skills for granted. When *reading skillfully*, however, you derive meaning from written words and symbols and evaluate their accuracy and validity. The approaches of skimming, scanning, and reading for detail can help you become a more skillful reader. First, skim until you find the portion of the document likely to contain the information you seek. Next, scan to locate the specific piece of information. When you find the information you are looking for, read for detail.

Skim to Get an Overview

To **skim** is to quickly glance through material to get an overview. Skimming is also known as *prereading*. You might choose to skim a chapter in a text to see what is in it before you actually read it. When skimming a document, notice headings, key words, phrases, and visual elements. The goal of skimming is to get a sense of the main ideas and scope of the content. Skimming is especially useful when you want to do any of the following:

- read for general information
- review the general coverage or content
- preview something you must later read in greater detail
- locate a specific section of a long document

Figure 7-1 Follow these suggestions for skimming material to get an overview of the information.

Skimming

- Read the title.
- Read section titles and headings. Use the table of contents if there is one.
- Note sections that are boxed, bulleted, numbered, or set in different typefaces.
- Identify words in the body of the content that are underlined, italicized, boldfaced, or in all capital letters.
- Look for information that is called out, such as a bulleted list.
- Flip through pages, spending no more than 10 to 15 seconds on each page.
- Look at visuals and their captions.
- Review summaries if they are included.

Goodheart-Willcox Publisher

Skimming is a fast process. One of the most important reasons for skimming is to help you prioritize your work. By skimming through your assignments, you get a glance at the topics covered and the length of the material. This can help you determine which assignments you may need to dedicate more time to read. Figure 7-1 shows suggestions for skimming.

Scan for Specific Information

To **scan** means to quickly glance through material to find specific information. *Skimming* is used when you are not sure what is in the material. *Scanning* is used when you know the information you need is there and you just have to find it. You might scan when you want to find any of the following:

- a vocabulary term that you know is in a certain chapter
- a word in a dictionary or an index
- an answer to a review question

If you scan too quickly, however, you are likely to miss the item for which you are looking. Figure 7-2 demonstrates suggestions for scanning.

Read for Detail

To **read for detail** is to read all words and phrases, consider their meanings, and determine how they combine with other elements to convey ideas. Other elements might include sentences, paragraphs, headings, or graphics. Reading for detail is also known as *reading for comprehension*.

Figure 7-2 Follow these suggestions for scanning material when locating specific information.

Scanning

- Determine the specific information for which you are searching.
- Observe how the information is structured such as in paragraphs or in lists.
- Determine clues or characteristics that will help locate the information.
- Look briefly each time there is an item with characteristics matching the search criteria. If it is not what you need, continue scanning.
- Quickly read surrounding material to determine whether an item is the exact information for which you are scanning.

Goodheart-Willcox Publisher

Figure 7-3 Follow these suggestions when reading material for detail.

Reading for Detail

- Anticipate the content and purpose for reading based on prior knowledge.
- Read phrase by phrase, connecting smaller concepts to form larger ideas.
- Question and comment on the author's statements while checking your understanding and comprehension of the material.
- Reread until you understand, or read ahead to see if later text provides clarity.
- If you get stuck on words or concepts, use prior knowledge to work through the problem areas or seek help from a friend or reference materials.
- When you finish reading for detail, evaluate and analyze what was read, considering the purpose of the information.
- Draw conclusions about the reading based on the purpose and situation, putting biases and emotions aside.

Goodheart-Willcox Publisher

This approach is what most people think of when they hear the word *reading*. Reading for detail is necessary when you read a textbook chapter to learn the concepts being taught. Generally, the process of reading for detail involves using the steps shown in Figure 7-3.

SQ3R

SQ3R, also called *SQRRR*, is a reading strategy to help readers retain written information. When you study for a test, it is important to comprehend what you are reading. SQ3R is useful for helping improve comprehension. There are five steps of the strategy: survey, question, read, recite, and review.

1. *Survey.* Skim, or preread, the material to look for any important headings, words, or figures. If there is a summary at the end of the chapter, reviewing it before you read the chapter can be helpful.

2. *Question.* Turn each heading into a review question. As you read each section, see if you can answer the question you created.

3. *Read.* Actively read the material, remembering to process the words, phrases, and sentences you read.

4. *Recite.* Recite what you read. Use your own words and summarize what you have read. If you cannot recite what you covered, read it again.

5. *Review.* Reviewing the material will help keep it fresh in your mind. If you are reading a chapter and know you will eventually be assessed on the content, review the material every few days. This will help make studying for the test easier and more effective than cramming would be.

General Reading Techniques

Your reading skills and habits were probably set years ago. If your reading skills are in need of improvement, you can strengthen them by practicing. Read as much as you can, and challenge yourself to apply the principles of active reading. If you strive to actively read, the more you read, the better you will become. Some general reading techniques that might improve your active reading skills include using prior knowledge, reading phrases instead of words, and marking your reading materials.

The reading strategy you decide to use is dependent on your learning style and which method works best for you.

Use Prior Knowledge

Your prior knowledge of a topic allows you to make sense of new information quickly. Recalling prior knowledge to aid reading works at all levels of the thought process. As you think about the content you are reading, attach new knowledge to prior knowledge, and act accordingly. A similar use of prior knowledge in reading takes place at the word or conceptual level. If you come across unfamiliar words or groups of words, you can often figure out meanings by recalling their usage in other contexts.

Read Phrases, Not Words

Active readers read groups of words rather than individual words. Reading word by word is slow, reduces concentration, and reduces the ability to connect concepts to form meaning. Words combine to make meaningful phrases. Many words have significant meaning only when combined with other words to form phrases. Some words acquire new meaning when attached to other words.

Read the following sentence one word at a time:

> One of the companies that submitted a bid for this project is Dean & Brown Contracting.

Now read the same sentence in meaningful phrases:

> One of the companies / that submitted a bid / for this project / is Dean & Brown Contracting.

Reading in phrases requires concentration and steady practice. If you find that you do not already read in phrases, practice this technique. This change in the way you read will help you read faster and improve understanding at the same time.

Mark Reading Materials

Making annotations and highlighting reading material are effective reading techniques. An **annotation** is a note or comment added to a document to help explain its contents. Annotations will help you better understand and remember what you have read. You will also be able to identify questions that come up as you read.

Always have a pen ready to use when you read. Write annotations in the margins in the form of notes, questions, or comments. If you need to write notes but do not want to mark directly on the material, use self-stick notes instead. Use stick-on tabs to mark pages you will use repeatedly.

Highlight or underline important text. *Highlighting* information involves marking text with a bright, easily seen color. It helps you focus while reading and remember what you read. When you need to refer back to the material in the future, you can scan for the highlighted information and find it easily.

When reading skillfully, meaning is derived from written words and symbols.

Yakobchuk Viacheslav/Shutterstock.com

Improving Your Reading Skills

The average student reads 250 words per minute. If you are a slow reader or wish to enhance your reading skills in general, now is the time to correct this. Reading more and using a dictionary are the best ways to improve your reading skills.

By reviewing your reading habits, you can look for the areas where your skills need improvement. Here are some suggestions for improving how effectively you read.

- Time yourself. How long does it take you to read and understand a section of text or a chapter of a book? If it takes you longer than average, read more to practice.

- Pay attention to how often you interrupt yourself before you finish reading something. If this happens frequently, look for factors that might be the cause, eliminate the distractions, and work on staying focused.

- Pay attention to your thoughts as you read. If you think about something other than what you are reading, you will not remember what you have just read.

- Recognize whether you read word by word or phrase by phrase. Practice reading in phrases.

- Keep track of the number of times you do not fully understand what you just read after you have completed a page. Analyze why this is happening, and use the information in this chapter to try to correct it.

Most classes require that students enroll in a digital course, use an online text, or read supplemental materials online. Reading on a screen, however, can have a negative effect on student comprehension. The temptation to multitask rather than focus on the material can be challenging when completing an online assignment. The tendency to skim through digital screens and ignore the details sometimes interrupts the process of comprehension. To improve your reading skills when studying online, apply the same suggestions as noted above for reading print. In addition, consider the following suggestions.

- Adjust the zoom of the screen to make it easier to see words and comprehend meaning.

- If videos are embedded in the content, take time to view them. The material will help add clarification to understanding what you are reading.

- Take advantage of annotation or highlighting features of the program to note important terms or content.

- If there is an audio feature for terms or other content, listen for reinforcement.

If you feel that you need professional help to improve your reading skills, a class on reading comprehension or time management might be the answer for you. Libraries and schools usually offer classes for reading improvement.

Reading assignments should not be taken lightly if you want to pass the tests you will be required to take. Some students have the idea that they can go to class, listen, take notes, ignore reading assignments, and still get a good grade on a test. This might work sometimes, but it is not a good plan if you want to be successful throughout your years in school and earn a degree.

SUMMARY

- **(LO 7-1) Describe active reading.**
  Active reading is processing the words, phrases, and sentences you read. Active reading requires the reader to use strategies to understand the material so comprehension is possible.
- **(LO 7-2) Explain how skimming, scanning, and reading for detail can help a person become a skillful reader.**
  Skimming is used when you are not sure what is in the material. *Scanning* is used when you know the information you need is there and you just have to find it. To *read for detail* is to read all words and phrases, consider their meanings, and determine how they combine with other elements to convey ideas.
- **(LO 7-3) Define SQ3R and the five steps of this strategy.**
  SQ3R is a reading strategy to help readers retain written information. There are five steps of the strategy: survey, question, read, recite, and review.
- **(LO 7-4) Identify examples of general reading techniques.**
  Some general reading techniques that might improve your active reading skills include using prior knowledge, reading phrases instead of words, and marking your reading materials.
- **(LO 7-5) Summarize strategies to improve reading skills.**
  By reviewing your reading habits, you can look for the areas where your skills need improvement. Some tips for improving how effectively you read include timing yourself, paying attention to how often you interrupt yourself, paying attention to your thoughts as you read, recognizing whether you read word by word or phrase by phrase, and keeping track of the number of times you do not fully understand what you just read.

GLOSSARY TERMS

Visit the G-W Learning companion website at **www.g-wlearning.com/careereducation/** to review the following glossary terms.

active reading	read for detail
prior knowledge	SQ3R
skim	annotation
scan	

REVIEW

1. Describe active reading.

2. Explain how skimming, scanning, and reading for detail can help a person become a more skillful reader.

3. When is skimming a useful technique to use when reading?

4. When is scanning a useful technique to use when reading?

5. What does it mean to read for detail?

6. List and briefly explain each step of SQ3R.

7. Identify examples of general reading techniques.

8. How does prior knowledge help when reading?

9. Discuss ways to mark reading materials.

10. Summarize strategies to improve reading skills.

CRITICAL THINKING

1. Active reading requires the reader to use different strategies to understand the material. What strategies could you use to become a better active reader?

2. Explain when you typically use skimming and scanning when studying.

3. Self-monitoring your reading skills is a way of self-questioning to make sure you understand what you are reading. What are some self-questions you can ask yourself to increase your reading comprehension?

4. Review the steps of SQ3R listed in this chapter. How do you see yourself implementing this reading technique in your studies?

5. What are some actions you can take now to improve your reading skills?

INTERNET ACTIVITY

Annotation Techniques. Using the Internet, research *how to annotate text when reading.* Which techniques are commonly used? Did you learn about any new ones? Write a brief summary of the techniques you researched. Then choose a method for annotating your readings, such as color-coding, and briefly explain how you will use it when reading.

Digital Devices. Most classes require that students read a textbook or supplementary material in a digital format. However, reading on digital devices poses certain challenges. Using the Internet, research *challenges of reading on digital devices.* Summarize the impact that reading on a screen has on reading comprehension. What can you do to overcome these challenges?

SKILLS PRACTICE

Visit the G-W Learning companion website at **www.g-wlearning.com/careereducation/** to access and complete the following study skills practice activities:

Study Skills Activity 7-1 Improving Your Reading Skills. Active reading requires the reader to use strategies to understand the material so comprehension is possible. Open the 7-1 file and read the passage. After you have finished, answer the questions that follow.

Study Skills Activity 7-2 SQ3R. SQ3R is a reading strategy to help readers retain written information. Open file 7-2, reread this chapter, and record your responses to each step. Keep this checklist at hand to use when reading future chapters.

CHAPTER 8

Becoming an Active Listener

Photographee.eu/Shutterstock.com

BEFORE YOU READ

Before you begin reading this chapter, see what you already know about active listening by taking a pretest. The pretest is available at **www.g-wlearning.com/careereducation/**

LEARNING OUTCOMES

On completion of this chapter, prepare to:

8-1   Describe active listening.

8-2   Explain purposes for listening.

8-3   Identify examples of techniques to become a better listener.

Active Listening

How well do you listen? Do you hear what your instructors are saying when they are lecturing, or are you daydreaming? Listening is one of the most important skills an individual can develop. The ability to listen for information is a study skill necessary for academic and future success.

Hearing is a physical process. **Listening** is an intellectual process that combines hearing with evaluating. Just because you can hear a person speak does not mean you are listening to what is said. When you *listen*, you make an effort to process what you *hear*.

Active listening is the act of processing what a person says so the message can be comprehended. Active listeners know when to take notes, follow directions, comment, or remain quiet. Active listening can be achieved by applying the *listening process*. The steps in the listening process, as shown in Figure 8-1, are as follows.

- *Receive.* Focus on the sender and hear the message.

- *Decode.* Assign meaning to words and sounds so the message can be understood.

- *Remember.* Take time to remember what is being said so the information can be used.

- *Evaluate.* Apply critical-thinking skills to evaluate what was said.

- *Respond.* Give feedback to show that you received the message.

Active listeners know when to take notes, follow directions, comment, or remain quiet.

wavebreakmedia/Shutterstock.com

Listening with Purpose

Before you go to class, decide what information you hope to gain. Find out as much as you can about what you are going to hear before you arrive by reading an assignment or completing other homework. You will be a more effective listener if you can identify your purpose for listening and adapt your behavior accordingly.

Figure 8-1 Active listening can be achieved by applying the listening process.

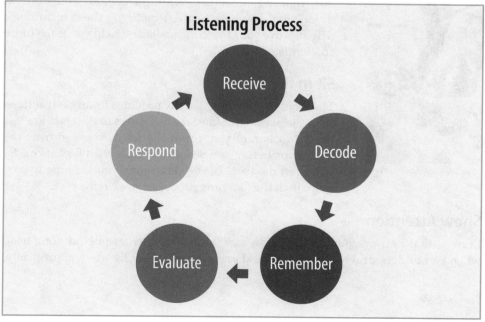

Goodheart-Willcox Publisher

As a student, one of the major purposes you have for listening is to hear what is being presented in a lecture. The lecture might be based on material you were assigned to read before coming to class. In this situation, your purpose is to listen and build on prior knowledge. *Prior knowledge* is experience and information a person already possesses. Alternatively, the lecture might be based on new material you are hearing for the first time. In this situation, your level of listening and purpose are focused on learning new content and unfamiliar terminology and concepts.

Another purpose for listening is to hear what is being said so you can take good notes while the instructor is lecturing. (Note taking is discussed in Chapter 9.) There are many times when a lecture includes information that *is not* in a textbook or perhaps provides additional background on content to support material that *is* in the textbook. The notes you take will more than likely be the only record of the material. If you lack good note-taking skills, your study materials will be less than sufficient when it comes time for a test.

A sometimes overlooked purpose for listening in class is paying attention to instructions. Most instructors will verbally relay specific details for submitting homework or projects, a change of class time or location, or other important information. If you do not listen for instructions, you may end up missing a class or an important due date for an assignment. Pay attention to verbal details that might affect your success as a student. Record them in your planner or notebook for future reference.

In addition, as you listen, try to anticipate your future needs. For example, determine whether you will need any additional information for assignments or questions answered after class. If so, request information such as the instructor's office hours or where to find a tutoring center. Record these resources in your planner so you can utilize them again should a future problem arise.

Use active listening techniques to become a better listener in class.

Tom Wang/Shutterstock.com

Listening Techniques

There are techniques you can use to help you focus and become a better listener in class. Some of these techniques are sitting in the front of the classroom, showing attention, fighting barriers, providing feedback, and summarizing what you have heard. Practicing these techniques will improve your listening skills and help you learn more efficiently.

Sit in the Front

The front of the room usually provides fewer distractions than the back of the classroom. Others in the class are less likely to distract you. From the front, you can hear the instructor better and see any visuals with less effort. By sitting in the front of the classroom, you are able to participate in the listening process more easily.

Show Attention

Convey that you are paying attention by facing the instructor. Nod your head when you understand what is being said and respond verbally when appropriate.

Be mindful that the instructor will be evaluating your responses. Nonverbal cues such as roving eyes, a slouched posture, and inappropriate facial expressions communicate indifference and even rudeness.

When fellow classmates contribute to the class discussion, be respectful, show attention, and listen to what they are saying. They may ask questions or offer information that may be helpful to your learning. Listen to what they are saying to build upon your prior knowledge and to avoid repeating questions or responses.

Fight Barriers

Good listeners fight barriers so they can focus their attention on the task of listening. A **barrier** is anything preventing clear, effective communication.

Internal barriers are distractions that occur within an individual such as fatigue, hunger, or wandering thoughts. *External barriers* are distractions that occur in the surrounding environment of an individual. Examples of external barriers can include looking out the window, watching the clock on the wall, or hearing noises outside of the classroom.

Be aware of the barriers that might interfere with good listening. Concentrate on the lecture or discussion in class to keep distractions created by one's own mind in check.

Provide Feedback

When possible, provide feedback to the instructor by asking questions and making comments. This demonstrates that you have been actively listening. Most instructors welcome friendly questions asking for clarification or further information. Feedback provides an opportunity to repeat or elaborate on a point.

- *Ask questions at the appropriate time.* Avoid interrupting a lecture. Instead, write down questions or comments, and wait until the instructor invites them.

- *Be sure your question is relevant.* Avoid questions or comments not relating to the topic. If you need to discuss an unrelated topic, wait for that topic to come up in the lecture or approach the instructor after class has ended.

- *Limit the length of your question.* Keep your questions and comments short. Avoid getting into a long, one-on-one discussion with the instructor. Long discussions are inconsiderate and cut into time for other students to ask questions. If you need to pursue a discussion beyond a follow-up question or comment, do so after class.

Feedback is a valuable listening technique when used appropriately. It not only helps the person lecturing, it can help those in the audience gain clarification about information that has been presented. However, feedback should always be given with respect. Remember your role as a student and demonstrate politeness when offering feedback to your instructor.

Summarize

After the lecture has ended, write a brief summary of the information you learned. **Summarizing** is an active listening technique that entails writing or thinking about the main points that were heard. This action can help to ensure you fully understood what was being said without omitting any important details. The summary is an important part of your notes and will be helpful when studying for a test.

SUMMARY

- **(LO 8-1) Describe active listening.**
  Active listening is the act of processing what a person says so the message can be comprehended and can be achieved by applying the *listening process*.
- **(LO 8-2) Explain purposes for listening.**
  One of the major purposes for listening is to hear what is being presented in a lecture. Other purposes include listening to what is said to take good notes and paying attention to instructions.
- **(LO 8-3) Identify examples of techniques to become a better listener.**
  Some techniques to becoming a better listener are sitting in the front of the classroom, showing attention, fighting barriers, providing feedback, and summarizing what you have heard.

GLOSSARY TERMS

Visit the G-W Learning companion website at **www.g-wlearning.com/careereducation/** to review the following glossary terms.

hearing

listening

active listening

barrier

summarize

REVIEW

1. What is the difference between hearing and listening?

2. Describe active listening.

3. Define each step of the listening process.

4. How can a student prepare to listen in class?

5. Explain purposes for listening.

6. Identify examples of listening techniques.

7. Why is sitting in the front of the classroom a good listening technique?

8. Identify examples of nonverbal cues that communicate indifference or rudeness.

9. List suggestions for ways of providing feedback to an instructor.

10. What is the benefit of summarizing?

CRITICAL THINKING

1. Listening is one of the most important skills a person can learn. Discuss the importance of becoming a good listener and how you think it could potentially affect your grades as well as your personal life and future career.

2. Offering feedback in class is a signal that you are paying attention. Describe the approach and technique you use when giving feedback to an instructor or classmate.

3. Where do you normally sit when you come to class? On what do you base this decision? How does it affect your listening skills?

4. Recall a time when a listening barrier affected your learning. Describe the barrier and how it could have been avoided. How will you avoid listening barriers in the future?

5. Name and describe your strongest listening technique.

INTERNET ACTIVITY

Listening Types. There are five types of active listening. Using the Internet, research each type: *appreciative listening, critical listening, deliberative listening, empathic listening,* and *reflective listening*. Think of a time when you applied each type of listening. Reflect on how well you listened during each situation. In which type of listening do you excel?

SKILLS PRACTICE

Visit the G-W Learning companion website at **www.g-wlearning.com/careereducation/** to access and complete the following study skills practice activities:

Study Skills Activity 8-1 Listening Skills. Listening is an important study skill that can help a person be a more effective learner. Open the 8-1 file and rate your listening skills.

Study Skills Activity 8-2 Improving Your Listening Skills. Active learning can be achieved by using the listening process. Open the 8-2 file. Choose one of your instructors' oral lessons. Identify and analyze the listening process for this lesson.

CHAPTER 9

Improving Your Note Taking

wavebreakmedia/Shutterstock.com

BEFORE YOU READ

Before you begin reading this chapter, see what you already know about note taking by taking a pretest. The pretest is available at **www.g-wlearning.com/careereducation/**

LEARNING OUTCOMES

On completion of this chapter, prepare to:

9-1   Define note taking.

9-2   Summarize taking notes in class.

9-3   Discuss reviewing notes taken in class.

9-4   Summarize taking notes from print sources.

A first rule of taking notes is to practice active listening.

wavebreakmedia/Shutterstock.com

Note Taking

Note taking is the process of writing key information from a lecture, text, or other sources on paper or a digital device. Well-written notes provide a record of important information you learned in a lecture or at a presentation. These notes, along with your textbook, can serve as a resource when studying for a test or completing assignments.

As a student, you have the responsibility to attend class, pay attention, learn, and take good notes. Your instructor provides handouts, visuals, and explanations to help you understand the subject matter. Taking notes on the interactions and conversations that happen in class can be beneficial to your education. It is unwise to think that you can read the text, skip class, and pass a test. Attendance must be a priority.

You are responsible for reading and studying the text as well as listening to the instructor. A lecture typically includes material *from the text* and important information *not in the text*. This is one reason good note taking is important. If the lecture information is not in your notes, you will not have it to review when it comes time to study for a test. This is another good reason for not skipping class.

When you go to class, be prepared to take notes. Opt for a seat close to the front of the room so you can hear well and see visuals clearly. This will help you focus and be less distracted than you would be sitting in the back of the room.

If handwriting lecture information works for you, loose-leaf paper inside a three-ring binder is preferable to a spiral-bound notebook. Three-ring binders allow for more organizational freedom than traditional notebooks as you can easily insert and remove documents. You can include handouts, such as the course syllabus, in the binder along with your notes. If you prefer a spiral-bound notebook, consider using one with pockets to store handouts or other materials. This will help keep you organized.

Before the class starts, write the name of the course, instructor, date, or other information on the first page of the notes as an identifier. Easy ways to organize notes are by date or subject. Headings, subheadings, titles, and subtitles can save time when reviewing for a test.

When you take your seat, be ready to write. Remove paper, pens, highlighters, or other items you might need out of your backpack and place them on the desk. It is rude to rummage through personal items when the lecturer has started.

Some students prefer to use a laptop or tablet to take notes instead of pen and paper. This can be an effective method for taking notes if your keying skills are good. If a digital device is your preferred method of note taking, make sure to charge the battery before you go to class. Have the device on and ready to go as well as all e-mail and social media pages closed before the class starts. Consider disconnecting the Wi-Fi or using a web blocker to reduce online distractions during class.

Alternatively, if you are an auditory learner, you might consider recording the lecture. This requires planning and a visit to the instructor to request permission a minimum of one day before the class. It also necessitates your device to be working and ready to record as soon as the class begins.

There are extenuating circumstances when you might need to be absent from a class. When this happens, ask a fellow student to share notes and get you up to speed on what you missed. Using a classmate's notes is not as effective as being present and taking your own notes, but borrowed notes can be helpful. In addition, ask your instructor if he or she can spend some time tutoring you outside of class hours to get you up to speed.

Taking Notes in Class

Taking notes is a hands-on activity, which means you are practicing active learning. **Active learning**, similar to active reading and active listening, means fully participating in activities that lead to understanding of content or information. When you take notes, you hear the words of the speaker or see the examples on the board. Then, you decide the important points and record them on paper or digital device to help with retrieving the information for future uses.

A first rule of taking notes is to practice active listening as presented in Chapter 8. You must not only hear what is said but also comprehend, evaluate, and translate or summarize the information. Then, determine if the material is important enough to write down. One way to determine importance is repetition by the lecturer. If the person lecturing repeats something, it must be important so write it down.

When taking notes, discretion must be used to decide which key words or main ideas are important so that they can be recorded. It is not practical to write down every word that is said in a lecture. To facilitate the process, some students use their own version of shorthand. **Shorthand** is rapid writing using abbreviations and symbols. Establishing a routine of abbreviations for common words enables you to focus on the important information that needs to be noted.

Selecting a note-taking system is a personal preference and should be chosen based on your needs. You have been taking notes in class for years and your system might work fine for you. Be objective and evaluate your current practices as there may be ways to fine-tune what you are doing. Take time to investigate some well-known systems that follow.

- *Cornell System.* The Cornell System is a method in which notes are organized into three sections: left side for main ideas or key terms, right side for main points and details, and bottom for a summary.

- *Mapping.* Mapping involves the use of visuals to show the relationship between topics. Notes are organized by the main topic at the top or middle of the page with subtopics branching out and important notes underneath each subtopic. This system is especially useful for visual learners.

- *Charting.* Charting is a system of using columns to organize a large amount of facts. Notes are divided into columns based on number of main topics with subtopics placed underneath.

- *Sentence note taking.* Sentence note taking is useful for recording large amount of information quickly. Main topics are placed as headings followed by subtopics in quick and simple sentences.

- *Outlining.* Outlining is a more common form of note taking. It is used to organize a large amount of detail into headings with subtopic bullet points.

Whichever method you decide to use, stick with it. Each page of notes should appear similar to the others. Neatness does not count here, but make sure you can read what you are writing. Do not worry about misspelled words, grammar, or punctuation when you are taking notes. You can correct errors when you review the notes after you leave class.

Figure 9-1 Consider these suggestions when taking notes in class.

Taking Effective Notes

- Be selective. Write down only what is important and what you might not remember.

- Organize your notes as you write, if possible. Let the format of your notes correspond to the instructor's message.

- Use abbreviations and symbols. If the notes are for you only, cut as many corners as you like as long as the notes remain useful.

- Avoid repeating information that appears in a handout. Highlight or put a check mark in the margin of the handout to remind yourself of key points.

- Write down the main point of any visual aids. If a visual aid includes data you need later, write down the source or ask the instructor afterwards for a copy of the visual.

- Ask questions if something is not clear. Notes are ineffective if they lack clarity.

- Many times an instructor summarizes the most important points at the end of a lecture. This is a good time to be listening carefully with a pen ready.

Goodheart-Willcox Publisher

Note taking is a skill that will be used in one's personal life as well as a career. It is not a substitution for active listening but a tool to facilitate learning. Suggestions for taking effective notes are shown in Figure 9-1.

Reviewing Your Notes

Soon after class, review your notes. Make sure you can read your writing and that what you put on paper makes sense. If needed, take the time to reorganize your notes. If time permits, compare your notes with a fellow student to make sure all the key points of the lecture are noted.

Consider creating flash cards or graphic organizers of the important points from your notes. While information is fresh in your mind, you can note important facts, items for which you need extra time to study, or other content which you need reinforcement. These will serve as great study tools when prepping for a test.

Study your notes. In addition to reviewing your notes for accuracy, create a routine of studying them before the next class meets. This routine serves three important purposes.

- It enables you to ask questions in the next class about concepts you did not quite understand or on which you need clarification.

- It helps you be prepared to relate your prior knowledge to what is presented in subsequent classes.

- It helps you build knowledge so when test time comes, you feel confident about what you have learned and makes test preparation more efficient.

Studying your notes after class helps you remember what was presented in the lecture. When it comes time for a test, you will be more confident and prepared. A checklist for reviewing notes is shown in Figure 9-2.

Taking Notes from Print Sources

Most instructors create tests using information from class lectures as well as the textbook or other reading assignments noted on the class syllabus. Therefore, writing notes while reading a class assignment is an important skill to develop.

Figure 9-2 Consider these strategies for reviewing your notes after class.

Strategies for Reviewing Notes

- Review notes within 24 hours of class.
- Rewrite any information that is difficult to read.
- Insert any additional information that you recall while the lecture is still fresh in your mind.
- Highlight, underline, or mark main points that will help you prepare for a test.
- Compare notes with a classmate to make sure all key points are noted.
- Recite notes aloud in your own words to assess the amount of information you have retained.

Goodheart-Willcox Publisher

Taking notes from a textbook requires some of the same practices required for taking notes in a lecture. Before you start reading printed material, be prepared by having paper and a pen or pencil or your laptop set up and ready to work.

Label your notes by recording the name of the text or source material, chapter number, and chapter title at the top of the page. Consider including the page numbers from the book as a reference if you need to go back to review a part of the chapter or refer to a visual.

When you begin reading, apply the strategies you learned in Chapter 7. Skim a chapter before you read it so you know what to anticipate. *Skim* is to quickly glance through material to get an overview. Pay attention to headings and subheadings. This will give you a general sense of the information included in the chapter. The goal of skimming, or prereading, is to get a sense of the main ideas and scope of the content.

Next, scan the chapter. To *scan* means to quickly glance through material to find specific information. Scanning the pages and reading the first sentence of each paragraph will help you understand the key points discussed in the chapter. Take notice of any words that are highlighted or in bold print. If there are illustrations, charts, or graphs, review them as well. They can provide additional information and clarify the content in the chapter.

After you have scanned a chapter, break it into smaller sections. Apply active reading strategies while reading one section at a time. *Read for detail* and identify key points, important facts, and vocabulary. This is when reading comprehension is the focus.

When you begin taking notes from print sources, use a note-taking system that works for you. It may be similar to the one you use for taking notes during a lecture. Be selective about what you write down. Taking effective notes requires finding the right balance between writing too many notes and writing too few. When you come to the end of a section, write a brief summary in your own words. Paraphrasing information helps you understand it as you write it down.

When reading a textbook, review and complete end-of-chapter questions or activities to help recall and review the main topics or key points of a chapter. Your notes should include enough information to complete the activities.

When you finish a chapter of reading of the text, compare your notes with your lecture notes. Note the similarities and differences of information that you learned from both sources.

Taking notes from a textbook requires some of the same practices required for taking notes in a lecture.

lightpoet/Shutterstock.com

SUMMARY

- **(LO 9-1) Define note taking.**
  Note taking is the process of writing key information from a lecture, text, or other sources on paper or a digital device. Well-written notes provide a record of important information learned in a lecture or at a presentation. These notes, along with a textbook, can serve as a resource when studying for a test or completing assignments.

- **(LO 9-2) Summarize taking notes in class.**
  Taking notes in class begins with active listening and deciding which key words or main ideas are important to write down. Developing a system of shorthand enables a student to focus on the important information that needs to be noted. In addition, it is helpful to select a note-taking system that should be chosen based on an individual's needs and to stick with that method.

- **(LO 9-3) Discuss reviewing notes taken in class.**
  Review notes soon after class. Review handwriting and that all information makes sense. If needed, reorganize notes. In addition, compare notes with a fellow student to make sure all key points of the lecture are noted. Consider creating flash cards or graphic organizers and taking the time to study lecture notes.

- **(LO 9-4) Summarize taking notes from print sources.**
  Have paper and a pen or pencil or laptop set up and ready to work. Label notes by recording the name of the text or source material, chapter number, and chapter title at the top of the page. When you begin reading, apply active reading strategies by skimming, scanning, and reading for detail. Use a note-taking system to record notes; it may be similar to the one used for lecture notes. Be selective and write down a brief summary in your own words for each section. When reading a textbook, review and complete end-of-chapter questions or activities. When finished, compare notes to lecture notes.

GLOSSARY TERMS

Visit the G-W Learning companion website at **www.g-wlearning.com/careereducation/** to review the following glossary terms.

note taking   shorthand
active learning

REVIEW

1. Discuss the importance of note taking.

2. Why is loose-leaf paper in a binder preferable to a spiral-bound notebook for note taking?

3. How can a person using a laptop be prepared to take notes?

4. If a student prefers to record a lecture rather than take written notes, what is the protocol?

5. Summarize taking notes in class.

6. List examples of note-taking systems to use during a lecture.

7. Explain how to review class notes.

8. What purpose does studying your notes before the next class serve?

9. In what ways is taking notes from print sources similar to taking notes in class?

10. Summarize the process of taking notes from printed sources.

CRITICAL THINKING

1. How would you describe your note-taking skills? Explain what you believe you do well and where you can improve.

2. Identify strategies you currently use for taking notes during a class lecture or presentation.

3. A fellow student is absent from class and wants to borrow your notes. Are you happy to share them or embarrassed? Expand on your reaction to the request.

4. In your own words, describe why you believe it is important to review your notes as soon as possible after the class is over.

5. Identify strategies you currently use for taking notes from your textbook or other reading material for class.

INTERNET ACTIVITY

Organizing Notes. Keeping your notes organized is just as important as writing notes. One option includes keeping separate binders for each class. Using the Internet, search *how to keep class notes organized*. Based on your search, explain how you will keep your notes organized.

SKILLS PRACTICE

Visit the G-W Learning companion website at **www.g-wlearning.com/careereducation/** to access and complete the following study skills practice activity:

Study Skills Activity 9-1 The Cornell System. The Cornell note-taking system is a note-taking method that provides a systematic format for condensing and organizing notes. This method divides notes into two columns: one for key points/questions the other for the notes. The bottom of the page provides a spot for summarizing the information. Open the 9-1 file and record your notes for a class using the Cornell note-taking system.

CHAPTER 10

Improving Your Memory

ESB Professional/Shutterstock.com

BEFORE YOU READ

Before you begin reading this chapter, see what you already know about memory by taking a pretest. The pretest is available at **www.g-wlearning.com/careereducation/**

LEARNING OUTCOMES

On completion of this chapter, prepare to:

10-1 Summarize memory as a component of study skills.

10-2 Identify examples of techniques to improve memory.

10-3 Explain memory retrieval.

Memory enables an individual to store, recall, and apply information when needed.

VGstockstudio/Shutterstock.com

Memory

Memory is a key component of developing effective study skills. **Learning** is behavior that enables an individual to acquire information. **Memory** is the part of the mind where information is encoded, stored, and retrieved. It enables you to store information that you learn, recall it, and apply it when needed.

An individual has two kinds of memory: short-term and long-term. **Short-term memory** is where information is retained and recalled for a brief moment without rehearsal. It is what you are focusing on at the moment. You initially remember the information, but it might not be important to you, so you forget it quickly. **Long-term memory** is the storage of information for an extended period of time. Long-term memory is what you remember because you understand the concept and its importance to you. You are able to comprehend the material, so it stays with you. Learning requires long-term memory.

You can move items in short-term memory to long-term memory by learning the information. In earlier chapters, you read about reading for comprehension and listening with purpose. If you apply these concepts and learn the material, it will stay with you for a longer period of time, especially if you review the information frequently.

Improving Memory

As part of developing effective study skills, it is important to develop techniques to help commit material to long-term memory. A large portion of material that you are committing to memory is course content on which you will be informally assessed, such as day-to-day classroom discussions, and formally assessed, such as scheduled tests.

Your job as a student is to read, listen, and remember information so you can apply it in meaningful ways to your education. Some students try to memorize information, rather than comprehend and learn what they read or hear. To **memorize** is to recite material word-for-word. Memorization is helpful for basic information such as dates in history. When learning concepts or pages of information, however, it is impossible to memorize every word. Similar to taking good notes, you must be selective in what you are trying to remember. In addition, you must concentrate on the selected information and block out distractions to help improve retention.

Instead of memorizing, choose to learn. Each educational experience builds on another, so learning from one experience builds the foundation for the next one. When you learn new material, you commit the information to memory. The commitment is made because you chose to remember. This requires that you develop interest in the information you are committing to memory. If you are not interested in it, you will not give it the attention it needs. You must understand why you are taking time to remember and the benefits you will reap from the experience.

Each person has memory tricks that work for him or her. There are a number of techniques that can help you learn, as well as retain, information. Some of these methods are rote learning, mnemonics, and chunking.

Rote Learning

Rote learning is remembering through repetition. You probably used rote learning when you learned the alphabet, multiplication tables, or months of the year.

Remembering through repetition can be accomplished through different techniques.

- Listening to something repeatedly, such as audio books, lectures, or recordings

- Doing something by learning from a demonstration then repeating similar actions

- Reading information multiple times to further understand the material

The idea of rote learning is that you will be able to recite information the more you repeat it. The more you repeat something, the easier it will be to recall information.

Each person has his or her own technique to learn and retain information.

wavebreakmedia/Shutterstock.com

Mnemonics

Mnemonics are good memorization tools. A **mnemonic** is any learning technique that helps a person remember something. It often involves taking the first letter from each list item in a series and using those letters to make a memorable word or sentence. You can create an acronym, write a sentence or poem, or even create a rhyme.

Create an Acronym

Acronyms can be great tools for remembering. **Acronyms** are abbreviated words or names formed from the initial letters of other words. For example, you probably learned in a geography class that the acronym *HOMES* is a great way to remember the Great Lakes. *HOMES* stands for **H**uron, **O**ntario, **M**ichigan, **E**rie, and **S**uperior.

Huron
Ontario
Michigan
Erie
Superior

Write a Sentence or Poem

An **acrostic** is a made-up sentence or poem in which the first letter of each line of text spells out a word or message. For example, *My very eager mother just served us nectarines* is a common acrostic sentence for remembering the order of the eight planets in the solar system. The planets are **M**ercury, **V**enus, **E**arth, **M**ars, **J**upiter, **S**aturn, **U**ranus, and **N**eptune.

My	**M**ercury
Very	**V**enus
Eager	**E**arth
Mother	**M**ars
Just	**J**upiter
Served	**S**aturn
Us	**U**ranus
Nectarines	**N**eptune

Create a Rhyme

Finding a way to turn information into rhymes is an excellent way to remember facts, dates, and other important data. Some well-known examples include the following:

- In fourteen hundred and ninety-two, Columbus sailed the ocean blue.

- I before E, except after C.

- 30 days hath September, April, June, and November.

This method is relatively easy to do, provided you are able to find a rhyme for the necessary information.

Chunking

Chunking is a memorization method that involves breaking up long strings of information into shorter, more manageable chunks. A good example of chunking is the memorization of phone numbers. A full, ten-digit phone number is often broken up into two three-digit sections and one four-digit section. For example, if you are trying to remember the phone number (202) 555-1111, you will likely chunk it as 202, 555, and 1111. Most people do this without ever thinking about it. Chunking is effective, but it is limited in its scope. For example, it does not work well with facts such as a list of the amendments to the US Constitution and what each one accomplished. Such a list is too long to chunk.

Relearning how to skate is an example of using memory retrieval.

XiXinXing/Shutterstock.com

Memory Retrieval

As a student, you are enrolled in classes so you can learn information and become an educated individual. In each class, you commit information to memory that will be used when you are taking a test or completing other class assignments.

Memory retrieval is accessing information from long-term memory when it is needed. For example, when taking a final exam, you need to retrieve information from your memory in order to answer questions. If you simply memorized data early in the term, you may or may not be able to remember the information well enough to answer test questions. If you committed the material to memory, you will probably be able to recall it if certain triggers are available.

Memory retrieval also aids in retrieving past information and using it to build upon. When you first started school, you learned the basics, such as the alphabet. As you advanced, you retrieved the basics of letters from your memory to learn how to read words and write sentences. If you have comprehended and learned the material, you will continue to build on what you have learned so you can apply the information in your personal life and future career.

There are multiple ways in which information can be accessed from long-term memory.

- *Recall.* Recall means you are able to *remember* information. For example, you took a test and were able to remember enough information to insert a response for a fill-in-the-blank question.

- *Recognition.* Recognition is the ability to *recognize* information after seeing or experiencing it again. For example, you read an assignment once or twice. When you took the test, you were not able to write a short-answer response, but you were able to recognize the correct answer for a multiple-choice question.

- *Recollection.* Recollection means you are able to *reconstruct* information. For example, this semester you took good notes, read assignments, and prepared for each class. Before the test, you spent time reviewing materials and preparing. The test included essay questions for which you were able to recollect information from various memories to write a response to each question.

- *Relearning.* Relearning means to learn information already stored in memory for a second time. For example, you once knew how to skate. Since you have not skated in years, you relearn the basics so you can skate without falling.

Memory retrieval is a skill, but it is not always foolproof. We all experience problems remembering information. An important habit to establish for memory development is to learn to focus and pay attention to the task at hand. In addition, applying the techniques in this chapter will help make retrieving information from your memory more efficient.

SUMMARY

- **(LO 10-1) Summarize memory as a component of study skills.**
  Memory is a key component of developing effective study skills. *Memory* is the part of the mind where information is encoded, stored, and retrieved. It enables you to store information that you learn and recall and apply it when needed. *Short-term memory* is where information is retained and recalled for a brief moment without rehearsal. *Long-term memory* is the storage of information for an extended period of time.
- **(LO 10-2) Identify examples of techniques to improve memory.**
  There are a number of techniques that can help you learn, as well as retain, information. Some of these methods are rote learning, mnemonics, and chunking.
- **(LO 10-3) Explain memory retrieval.**
  Memory retrieval is accessing information from long-term memory when it is needed. It can help recall information from a person's memory in order to answer test questions. Memory retrieval also aids in retrieving past information and using it to build upon.

GLOSSARY TERMS

Visit the G-W Learning companion website at **www.g-wlearning.com/careereducation/** to review the following glossary terms.

learning	mnemonic
memory	acronym
short-term memory	acrostic
long-term memory	chunking
memorize	memory retrieval
rote learning	

REVIEW

1. Summarize memory as a component of study skills.

2. Explain the difference between short-term memory and long-term memory.

3. When is memorization helpful?

4. Identify examples of techniques to improve memory.

5. List examples of mnemonic devices.

6. Explain memory retrieval.

7. Discuss memory recall.

8. What is memory recognition?

9. Discuss memory recollection.

10. What does it mean to relearn from memory?

CRITICAL THINKING

1. Describe your ability to remember information. What techniques do you use when studying?

2. It is desirable to learn information rather than memorize. What is your opinion of memorizing for a test rather than learning the content?

3. Recall examples of mnemonic techniques you learned and list a few examples. How have mnemonics helped you retain information?

4. Recall a time when you successfully prepared for a test. Did the information stay with you? If so, how do you think you moved the information from your short-term memory to your long-term memory?

5. This text has provided information about multiple study skills. Describe how these skills you have learned can be applied to improving your personal memory retrieval ability.

INTERNET ACTIVITY

Memory Recall. Using the Internet, conduct a search on *memory recall*. Summarize your findings and discuss how this information can help you improve your study skills.

Short-Term vs. Long-Term Memory. Using the Internet, watch a news video about a current event. After you finish watching, write a brief summary of the video, including a list of specific details you learned. The next day, without referring to your notes, write down as much detail as you can recall from the video. Did you successfully transfer the information from short-term to long-term memory? Write several paragraphs explaining what you did to retain the information.

SKILLS PRACTICE

Visit the G-W Learning companion website at **www.g-wlearning.com/careereducation/** to access and complete the following study skills practice activity:

Study Skills Activity 10-1 Using Mnemonics. A mnemonic is any tool that helps us remember something. Remembering is an important study skill that can help a person be effective in school. Open the 10-1 file, and create mnemonic tools to help you remember the correct spellings of the words provided.

Test-Taking Strategies

Jasminko Ibrakovic/Shutterstock.com

BEFORE YOU READ

Before you begin reading this chapter, see what you already know about test-taking skills by taking a pretest. The pretest is available at **www.g-wlearning.com/careereducation/**

LEARNING OUTCOMES

On completion of this chapter, prepare to:

11-1 Explain how to prepare for a test.

11-2 Identify two common types of test questions.

11-3 Discuss take-home and open-book exams.

11-4 Summarize the process of taking an oral exam.

11-5 Describe the testing experience.

Preparing for a Test

Test or exam—what is the difference? Both terms refer to assessment and are sometimes used interchangeably. However, some instructors differentiate the terms. An instructor might consider a *test* as interim assessment administered during the course. Test grades are averaged and counted as a percentage of the overall grade. The same instructor may consider an *exam* as a summative assessment, such as a midterm or final, that carries more weight in a final grade. If you find an instructor using both terms, test and exam, ask for clarification. It will influence your preparation for each type of assessment. For instructional purposes, this chapter uses the terms interchangeably.

Preparing for formal assessment can be stressful, especially if you are taking a final exam at the end of a quarter, trimester, or semester. It would be great if you could attend a class, read the textbook, and get credit for the course without taking a test, but this is not the reality. Assessment is necessary to demonstrate that you understand and have mastered the subject matter. Test grades, especially final exams, are a primary validation and benchmark of what you have learned.

On the first day of class, your instructor probably distributed a syllabus for the course. Typically, test days are a part of the schedule so students know in advance when testing will occur. The syllabus may also include information on how test scores, along with class participation and other assignments, comprise the final grade for the course.

During a class before the test day, there more than likely will be a review of what will be covered on the test. This is an opportunity for you to ask what types of questions will be included as well as the amount of material you are expected to review. Take advantage of it and ask any questions that will help you prepare to study.

Test taking is important to your academic success. Therefore, it is necessary to apply the study skills you have learned in this text as you begin test preparation. Some good rules for test preparation include the following.

- Never wait until the night before to start studying for an important exam. Good time management suggests that you schedule multiple study sessions at least a week before the test.

- Define your study time. Decide the time of day you will study and how much time each day you will need to prepare for the test. Record the blocks of time on your calendar or planner. If you are part of a study group, arrange a time to meet.

- Identify where you will be studying. Keep in mind that if the campus library is your usual study area, it may be crowded during exam week and you may need an alternative location.

- Gather your notes, books, reference materials, and other study materials and be ready to focus.

In Chapter 9, you learned how to take effective notes. Now is the time to use those notes. Well-written notes provide information that might not be in the textbook, but might be on the test. In addition, if you have reviewed your notes after each class as suggested, you should have retained knowledge along the way and will not have to cram for the test.

Self-assess what you have learned and committed to memory. To **self-assess** means to evaluate what you have learned without the outcome of a grade. End-of-chapter questions, vocabulary terms, practice tests, and lab manuals that accompany some textbooks provide opportunities for self-assessment. Answering questions without using the text, and then using the text to confirm your responses,

Meeting with a study group is a helpful way to prepare for a test.

Rido/Shutterstock.com

Flash cards are helpful study tools especially when preparing for a language exam.

Eiko Tsuchiya/Shutterstock.com

is a great opportunity to assess your knowledge without the intimidation of a grade. Chances are good that if you complete all the activities accompanying a chapter in a text, you will do well on an exam.

Question Types

There are different types of questions that are typically included on assessments. Each type of question format requires a different approach for an answer and perhaps a different method of preparation. For example, a true/false question requires that when reading the question, you ascertain that all parts of the statement are true. If all parts are not true, then the answer must be false. When reading this type of question, you must be sure that you understand what is implied before you answer.

A typical test generally includes more than one type of question. In addition to true/false questions, you will most likely encounter multiple-choice and essay questions.

Multiple-Choice

Multiple-choice questions provide alternative answers for which the correct response is chosen. If you are not sure of an answer on a multiple-choice question, you have a good chance of making an educated guess about the correct one. Consider the following tips when answering multiple-choice questions.

- Read the question and try to answer it before looking at the answer choices. This will help you eliminate any answers you know are not true when you do look at the choices.

- Read all the choices for the question and eliminate all the ones that you know are incorrect. Understandably, incorrect answers can be eliminated immediately.

- Use the information from one question to help answer another question. Often answers from one question will help you answer another question as the information may overlap.

- Be aware that if the answer does not grammatically fit with the question, it is probably wrong.

- Check to see if two or more answers seem correct. If there is an "all of the above" or a variant of that answer, it might be a good option to select it.

If you have to guess at an answer, some general rules can apply. Highly specific or long answers can often be correct. But words like "always," "never," "must," "completely," or "only" often signal incorrect answers, since there are many exceptions to rules. Extreme answers are most likely incorrect.

Essay

An *essay question* evaluates student knowledge and ability to organize and express thoughts in a logical manner, analyze arguments, and critically think about information learned in class. An essay question may require a short-answer response that needs only a few sentences or phrases. Alternatively, it can require a more extensive answer of multiple paragraphs or pages. An essay response should resemble an essay that a student would write outside of class, with a clear thesis, organization, and correct grammar.

To prepare for essay questions, consider the following activities.

- Anticipate potential essay questions based on previous tests or class notes. You should be able to create a few practice questions.

- Ask your instructor if you can preview the essay questions before an exam. Some instructors may offer a list of potential questions as study prompts before a test.

- Practice writing your answers to the questions you have written or received from your instructor. This will help you estimate how much class time you need to answer certain questions and reinforce information you may need.

- Memorize facts, names, and events. Essay questions may require specific names and events in the answer. This will give you supporting information to put in your answer.

When answering essay questions during a test, keep these suggestions in mind to help you write the best possible response and prevent simple mistakes.

- Read all the questions carefully before you start writing.

- Write down all the information you remember for each question. This is called a "memory dump."

- Next, organize what you have written for the question. Avoid padding your answer with bluffing or unnecessary information.

- Finally, review what you have written. Look for misspellings, grammatical errors, or missing information.

A general rule for most exams is to avoid spending too much time on a single question. This applies especially when you are writing a lengthy response to an essay question. Move on and answer as many questions as you can, then go back to the questions to which you think you can add more information.

Take-Home and Open-Book Exams

You are probably most familiar with taking a test in a classroom with no resources permitted for reference. However, there are other options that an instructor might use. A *take-home exam* is an assessment that a student takes home to complete. An *open-book exam* is an assessment that allows students to use notes, books, or other materials to use as a reference during an exam taken in class. Take-home exams and open-book exams often overlap.

Students might think that take-home and open-book tests are easy, but they require preparation, just like any other assessment. Because resources can be used to answer the questions, instructors typically expect high-quality and well-structured responses and grade these tests more strictly. When completing a take-home or open-book test, consider the following points.

- Apply time-management techniques in the preparation and response strategies. A take-home test will have a deadline so plan accordingly. An open-book test with a time limit can become overwhelming when trying to look through multiple resources for answers.

- Study in advance. Just because you can take a test home or use resources for answers, it does not mean you should not study for it. If you only have a few hours to take the test, you do not want to waste time looking for answers you should know from basic studying.

- Be aware of what your instructor expects. These exams should be treated like other writing assignments.

- Create a good test-taking environment and stay organized with your resources. Carefully select the materials you require and organize them for quick reference.

Above all, exhibit academic integrity. Even though both types of exams allow resources to be used, the rules of cheating and plagiarism still apply.

Oral Exams

An *oral exam* is an assessment in which questions are answered in an interview format rather than by writing answers on paper. Oral exams are popular in foreign language courses, medical school, and other science-based courses. They are used to test the speaker's knowledge, presentation and speaking skills, and ability to communicate. They should be treated like an interview with formal dress, prepared answers, and expected follow-up responses.

There are two types of oral exams. *Formal oral exams* follow a prepared list of questions. There is a right and wrong answer, can be competitive, and permission must be requested to add related information that is not requested. *Informal oral exams* are more open and casual. Answers can be longer and the evaluation is more subjective than a formal oral exam. Value is added for problem solving, analysis, and presentation.

To prepare for a formal exam for a professional opportunity, talk to people who are in the field, have taken the exam, or classmates. Practice your answers with people who know the information to make sure that your answers are complete and correct. If you are using a presentation as part of the response, make sure to set up the equipment beforehand and practice with it to prevent mishaps.

During the exam, keep these suggestions in mind.

- Create a good impression by looking and acting professional. Dress appropriately and turn off distracting technology.

- The exam begins as soon as you walk into the room. Make sure to greet the instructor, introduce yourself, and give the instructor your full attention.

- Stay focused on the questions asked. Do not ramble. If you do not know the answer to a question, say so. Then, request permission to suggest an outline of how you would find the answer and solve the problem.

- Maintain composure even if you feel like the exam is not going well.

- Answer your questions with more than a "yes" or "no". You are trying to demonstrate your knowledge, so give evidence.

- When the exam is over, thank the instructor.

After the exam, follow up with the instructor. Just like with a job interview, thank the instructor again, summarize your performance, ask questions about the material and your overall performance, and note how you could do better next time.

Test Day

Make sure you get plenty of rest on the night before a test. On the day of a test, eat a healthy meal before you head off to class. Make sure you are well hydrated and avoid caffeine overload. Dress comfortably and wear layers. The room might get hot or cold, and if you are uncomfortable, it will affect your performance.

Make a restroom stop when you enter the building. Most instructors will not permit students to leave the classroom once the test has started. Arrive to the classroom at least five minutes before the test is scheduled to begin.

Depending on the type of test you are taking, you might be required to show identification when you arrive. If this is the case, make sure you have a driver's license, a student ID, or another form of identification with you. Bring pencils, pens, your laptop or tablet, or any other items your instructor requested. If you are using a digital device for the test, make sure the battery is fully charged and a cord is on hand, in the event you need one.

Review your notes one last time. If you created flash cards from your notes or a study guide, review them now. This will give you confidence and refresh your memory before the test begins.

Try not to worry. If you become overanxious, you might freeze and forget things you really know. Take a moment to breathe in and out slowly, relax, and believe in yourself. There is no reason to think you will not do well if you have prepared.

During the Test

The first action to take when you receive a test is to write your name on the appropriate designated line. Include any other information that might be requested, such as the date, class name, period, or time. If there are general instructions, read them completely. Do the instructions indicate a preference for pencil or ink? How does the professor expect you to write responses? Should you use scratch paper or can you write directly on the test? Is there a bubble sheet?

Next, quickly scan through the entire document to get an idea of the material covered. Ask the instructor clarifying questions if there is something you do not understand. Be aware of how much time you have to take the test and budget accordingly.

Test grades, especially final exams, are a primary validation and benchmark of what a student has learned.

Syda Productions/Shutterstock.com

If the test is delivered electronically, pay special attention to the submission process. Some tests do not permit the respondent to go back and review a question once the submit button is pressed. This is when reading skills are especially important. You do not want to disqualify a response because you failed to follow the directions.

As you read each question, do not assume you know what is being asked after reading only the beginning of it. Apply active reading skills and read the questions for detail. Complete the easiest questions and those worth the most amount of points first. This is the best way to ensure you receive a high point value. If you do not know an answer, skip the question and come back to it later. Allow enough time to write thoughtful responses if there are short-answer or essay questions.

Work at your own pace and ignore everything else around you. If there is time remaining after you have finished, take the opportunity to review your work. Make sure you have answered every question completely and to the best of your ability. Look for mistakes you might have made and proofread answers to any short-answer or essay questions. When you have completed the test and are satisfied with your work, submit it, and leave the testing room, if possible.

After the Test

After the test, reflect on the questions on which you think you did well and those on which you were not as successful as you would like to have been. Start with your study preparation. Did you apply the study skills you learned so you were prepared for the test? Next, review your physical being. Did you get enough sleep the night before and have a healthy meal the day of the test?

If you believe you lacked content preparation, perhaps a session with your instructor or a visit to a tutoring center might be helpful. This might be especially beneficial if the test you took was a midterm. Tutoring can help you perform better on the next test or on a final exam.

When your instructor returns your exam, review your performance. If the instructor reviews the exam and provides answers, take notes about what were expected as the answers. Sometimes, having an incorrect answer is as simple as it not being a *complete* answer. Knowing what your instructor considers to be a *complete* answer will help you on future exams. If you are unsatisfied with your grade, ask your instructor about makeup exams or extra credit. Save the exam so you can use it to study for future cumulative tests.

SUMMARY

- **(LO 11-1) Explain how to prepare for a test.**
  During a class before the test day, ask what type of questions will be included and the amount of material to review. Never wait until the night before to start studying for an important exam. Define study time and location. Gather notes, books, reference materials, and other study material and be ready to focus. Self-assess what you have learned and committed to memory.

- **(LO 11-2) Identify two common types of test questions.**
  A multiple-choice question provides alternative answers for which the correspondence is chosen. An essay question evaluates student knowledge and ability to organize and express thoughts in a logical manner, analyze arguments, and critically think about information learned in class.

- **(LO 11-3) Discuss take-home and open-book exams.**
  A take-home exam is an assessment that a student takes home to complete. An open-book exam is an assessment that allows students to use notes, books, or other materials to use as a reference during an exam taken in class. Both types of exams require preparation. Above all, students should exhibit academic integrity on these exams.

- **(LO 11-4) Summarize the process of taking an oral exam.**
  To prepare, talk to people who are in the field, have taken the exam, or classmates. Practice with people who know the information. During the exam, create a good impression. Answer the questions with more than "yes" or "no." When the exam is over, thank the instructor.

- **(LO 11-5) Describe the testing experience.**
  Eat a healthy meal, dress comfortably, and make a restroom stop before the test. Arrive at least five minutes before the test's start time. Bring all items requested, and review notes one last time. Scan the test to get an idea of the material covered and budget time accordingly. Complete the easiest questions and those worth the most amount of points first. Afterwards, reflect on the things that went well and those that were not as successful. When the test is graded and returned, review and ask for clarification from instructor if needed.

GLOSSARY TERMS

Visit the G-W Learning companion website at **www.g-wlearning.com/careereducation/** to review the following glossary terms.

self-assess

REVIEW

1. Compare and contrast the terms test and exam.

2. Explain how to prepare for a test.

3. Describe opportunities to self-assess when preparing for a test.

4. Identify two common types of test questions.

5. How can a student prepare for essay questions?

6. What are take-home and open-book exams?

7. List four strategies to consider when completing a take-home or open-book test.

8. Summarize the process of taking an oral exam.

9. Describe the testing experience.

10. What sources are available if a student believes they lacked content preparation for a test?

CRITICAL THINKING

1. Describe the steps you take when preparing for a test. Note how many days or weeks you begin to prepare and identify study techniques you use.

2. What are your test-taking strengths? What are your test-taking weaknesses?

3. Identify the type of test format with which you are most comfortable. What can you do to improve your test-taking skills for other types of tests that cause you to be uncomfortable?

4. How do you physically prepare for an important test?

5. Reflect on your last test-taking experience. Discuss how you typically evaluate a test you have just taken. How do you use an evaluation to prepare for the next test?

INTERNET ACTIVITY

Preparing to Take a Test. Fear of tests is called test anxiety. Sometimes the fear itself is enough to make test results worse. Using the Internet, conduct a search for *overcoming test anxiety*. Summarize strategies you learned that will help you the next time you have a test to take.

SKILLS PRACTICE

Visit the G-W Learning companion website at **www.g-wlearning.com/careereducation/** to access and complete the following study skills practice activity:

Study Skills Activity 11-1 Test-Taking Skills. Form a group with two or three other students. Conduct a discussion about how each of you typically prepare for exams. Open the 11-1 file. Record the different techniques your classmates use to study. What did you learn from this teamwork experience?

CHAPTER 12

Researching for College Papers

monticello/Shutterstock.com

BEFORE YOU READ

Before you begin reading this chapter, see what you already know about researching by taking a pretest. The pretest is available at **www.g-wlearning.com/careereducation/**

LEARNING OUTCOMES

On completion of this chapter, prepare to:

12-1 Differentiate between informal and formal papers.

12-2 Summarize secondary research and primary research.

12-3 Discuss intellectual property.

12-4 Explain how to credit sources used in a formal paper.

Researching for college papers is a skill that students need to develop for their academic career.

YanLev/Shutterstock.com

College Papers

During your educational years, you will be required to write many papers. A *college paper* is a document used to present information in a structured format to a specific audience for a defined purpose. Your instructors will require you to write papers in which you will provide facts and information from which conclusions are drawn.

An *informal* paper is a document that does not require formal research or documentation. Informal papers are typically short, no more than a few pages long. These papers can be written in the first person when the writer is reporting his or her own actions, conclusions, or ideas.

A *formal* paper is a document focusing on a broad main topic that is divided into subtopics for complete and clear coverage. These papers are often supported by formal research or gathering of information.

Research

Research is the process of investigation for the purpose of establishing facts and drawing conclusions. **Data** are the pieces of information gathered through research. Information usually falls into one of two categories: qualitative or quantitative data.

Qualitative data are the pieces of information that provide insight into how people think about a particular topic. This is data that cannot be measured with numbers. Qualitative data describes the qualities that something has or that someone feels. An example of qualitative data is a student's feelings after speaking with an instructor about a grade. The reaction could be rated on a scale from 1 to 10, but the score is not really concrete.

Quantitative data are the facts and figures from which conclusions can be drawn. This is data that can be measured with numbers. An example of quantitative data is the number of students who requested to speak with an instructor after a test. A specific number can be counted and reported.

There are two categories of research where data can be gathered: primary and secondary. For most formal writing, you will conduct secondary research first to find credible information. If the information is not found, primary research can be conducted.

Secondary Research

Secondary research is data someone else already assembled and recorded. There are many sources available, so take advantage of the opportunities to gather information. A wealth of information is available in print and online.

When conducting research online, use search engines to find reliable statistics and reports related to your topic. Major publications, trade and industry organizations, and government agencies often publish statistics and reports. Educational institutions, private industry organizations, and news outlets are also generally reliable Internet sources.

Since there are many websites available, it is important to start by narrowing your search. Decide the specific information you need, and then determine keywords to use in your search. It is usually best to be very specific at first. Expand the search by being less specific if the search does not turn up enough hits.

Another way to search is to look for a specific source of information. Sources might be familiar to you because they are well-known or well-respected publications, authors, organizations, journalists, bloggers, or news sources. These sources publish information by writers whose credentials can be verified. Ask yourself these questions.

- What are the author's credentials?
- What is the reputation of the publication in which the source material appears?
- Is the source a mainstream publication or an unknown?
- Is the information current?
- What is the copyright date?
- If data are presented, how were they collected, and what is the source?
- Can the information be validated through other sources?

When you conduct secondary research, consider the reliability and credibility of the sources you use. It is important to use accurate and complete information.

Primary Research

Primary research is first-hand research conducted by the writer in preparation for writing a paper. Primary research is usually conducted only if previously published data are not found. The most common methods of primary research for a paper are interviews, surveys, and observation.

When conducting surveys as a research tool, it is necessary to have a representative sampling of respondents chosen to participate.

Natee K Jindakum/Shutterstock.com

Interviews

Interviews are an effective method of getting information about people's opinions on topics. Some papers can benefit from qualitative information, such as individuals' attitudes, behaviors, motivations, or cultural backgrounds. In these cases, interviews are a good means for primary research.

Interviews can be conducted in groups or individually. One type of group interview is a focus group. A **focus group** is a small group of people with which the interviewer leads a discussion to gather answers to a set of questions. Focus groups are a good way to evaluate services or test new ideas. Typically, participants are asked about their perceptions, opinions, beliefs, and attitudes. The leader or another appointed person records the comments the participants make. It is crucial to the success of the interview to have detailed and accurate notes. Some focus groups use video equipment or sound recorders to capture the actual discussions.

One-on-one interviews can be used to gather the same type of information collected in a focus group. Depending on the topic, individual interviews might yield better information. For example, if your research is focused on adequate meal choices in the campus dining hall, a one-on-one interview may reveal more specific detail than a large group.

Surveys

A **survey** is a set of questions posed to a group of people to determine how that group thinks, feels, or acts. Surveys are often used to obtain quantitative data. When writing a survey, it is important to develop questions in a format that encourages responses. Figure 12-1 offers suggestions for writing survey questions.

Your success with a survey depends on identifying a representative sampling of respondents chosen to participate. A **representative sampling** is a group including a cross section of the entire population the researcher is targeting. Surveys conducted by professional organizations, such as political polls, use complex formulas and methods to identify representative samplings.

Observation

Observation is the process of watching people or situations and taking notes of what is going on around them. The key to observation is to make sure the subjects are unaware that they are being observed. Behaviors must be authentic and not influenced by the person watching them. When observation is used, objectivity is important. Objectivity is to be free of any biases. The researcher must observe and record information without personal prejudices.

Intellectual Property

When performing research, you must respect intellectual property. **Intellectual property** is something that comes from a person's mind, such as an idea, an invention, or a process. Intellectual property laws protect a person's or a company's inventions, artistic works, and other intellectual property.

The Internet provides countless sources for obtaining text, images, video, audio, and software. Even though this material is easily obtainable, this does not mean it is available for you to use any way you choose. Laws exist to govern the use of media and creative works. The creators or owners of this material have certain legal rights.

Plagiarism is claiming another person's material as your own, which is both unethical and illegal. If you must refer to someone else's work, follow intellectual property laws to acquire the information ethically. Use standard methods of citing sources. Citation guidelines in *The Chicago Manual of Style*, the Modern Language Association's *MLA Handbook*, and the *Publication Manual of the American Psychological Association* can be helpful.

Figure 12-1 Follow these guidelines when creating a survey.

Creating a Survey

- Make the questions easy to answer. Write questions that have a choice of answers, such as yes/no, multiple choice, or agree/disagree/strongly agree/strongly disagree. These are known as closed-ended questions and make it easy for the responder to answer. Open-ended questions that are subjective take more time to answer and evaluate.

- Write objective questions. Write questions that do not lead respondents to a particular answer. Biased questions produce biased data.

- Put the questions in a logical sequence. Group items, and when possible, label them with headings.

- Keep the survey short. If you ask too many questions, the respondent may not want to take the time to complete the survey.

- Include space for comments. Often the best information comes from unstructured responses.

Goodheart-Willcox Publisher

Piracy is the unethical and illegal copying or downloading of software, files, or other protected material. Examples of protected material include images, movies, and music. Piracy carries a heavy penalty, including fines and incarceration.

Copyright

A **copyright** acknowledges ownership of a work and specifies that only the owner has the right to sell the work, use it, or give permission for someone else to sell or use it. An idea cannot be copyrighted.

A copyright can be registered with the US Copyright Office, which is part of the Library of Congress. Published copyrighted material is often indicated by the © symbol or the statement "copyright by." Lack of the symbol or statement does not mean the material is not copyrighted.

All original material is automatically copyrighted as soon as it is in a tangible form. This means an essay is copyrighted as soon as it is written and saved or printed. Similarly, a photograph is copyrighted as soon as it is taken. Original material is protected legally whether or not the copyright is registered.

Any use of copyrighted material without permission is called **infringement**. Copyright laws cover all original work, whether it is in print, on the Internet, or in any other form of media. Scanning a document does not make the content yours.

Most information on the Internet is copyrighted, regardless if it is text, graphics, illustrations, or digital media. This means it cannot be reused without obtaining permission from the owner. Sometimes, the owner of the material places the material on the Internet for others to reuse. If this is not explicitly stated, however, assume the material is copyrighted and cannot be freely used.

Many websites list rules, called the *terms of use* or *terms of service*, which you must follow for downloading files. The terms of use agreement might come up automatically, for example, if you are downloading a file or software application. If, however, you are copying an image or a portion of text from a website, you need to look for the terms of use information.

Fair use doctrine allows individuals to use copyrighted works without permission in limited situations under very strict guidelines. This doctrine allows you to use copyrighted material for the purpose of describing or reviewing the work. A student writing about the material in an original paper is an example of fair use. Another example is a product-review website providing editorial comment. Fair use doctrine does not change the copyright or ownership of the material used under the doctrine.

Creative Commons

One popular method of allowing use of intellectual property is a Creative Commons (CC) license. A *Creative Commons (CC) license* is a specialized copyright license that allows free distribution of copyrighted work. Figure 12-2 shows the CC symbol that often appears on material bearing this license. If the creator of the work wants to give the public the ability to use, share, or advance his or her original work, a CC license provides this flexibility. The creator maintains the copyright and can specify how the copyrighted work can be used. For example, one type of CC license prohibits commercial use.

Public Domain

Public domain is material with no owner that can be used without permission. Material can enter the public domain when a copyright expires and is not renewed. Much of the material the federal, state, and local governments create is in the public domain. This is because taxpayer money is used to create this material. Additionally, the owner of a certain material might choose to give up ownership and place the material in the public domain.

Figure 12-2 The Creative Commons (CC) license allows free sharing of intellectual property.

Creative Commons

Crediting Sources

It is permissible to reference material from other writers provided proper credit is given. This is done by summarizing the work in your own words or by directly quoting part of it. If your paper includes information from sources you have researched, these sources should be acknowledged.

A **citation** lists the author, title, and publisher of the source; date of publication; and location of the publisher or online address. Citations can be listed in footnotes on the pages where the references occur or in a bibliography or works cited/references at the end of the paper.

The following information is needed for creating footnotes or a list of sources at the end of your paper:

- author's name
- publication title
- name and location of the publisher
- publication year
- website name, URL, and date of retrieval

Citing sources can follow three common formats: Modern Language Association's *MLA Handbook* (MLA), *American Psychological Association* (APA), and *Chicago Manual of Style* (Chicago Style). Your instructor will assign which format to follow. If not, ask your instructor which format to use for formal writing. These examples follow the Modern Language Association's *MLA Handbook*:

> **Book**
>
> [1]Stephen R. Srtatham, *Maintaining Time-Management: Effective Techniques to Make the Most of Your Time* (Simon & Smith Publisher, 2017) 91.

> **Online source**
>
> [2]Julie Street, The Importance of Sleep to Our Health–And How To Maintain a Healthy Sleep Schedule, Business Insider (2 April, 2018) http://www.businessinsider.com/how-to-maintain-a-healthy-sleep-schedule-2018-4

Footnotes should appear at the bottom of the page where the information is used. If you are placing your sources at the end of the paper, place them in either a bibliography or works cited. A bibliography lists all of the material you have consulted when writing your paper. A works cited/references only includes the list of items referenced in your paper.

SUMMARY

- **(LO 12-1) Differentiate between informal and formal papers.**
  An informal paper is a document that does not require formal research or documentation. Informal papers are typically short, no more than a few pages long. A formal paper is a document focusing on a broad main topic which is divided into subtopics for complete and clear coverage. These papers are often supported by formal research or gathering of information.

- **(LO 12-2) Summarize secondary research and primary research.**
  Secondary research is data someone else already assembled and recorded. It can be found online or in print. *Primary research* is first-hand research conducted by a writer in preparing for composing a paper. It is usually only conducted if previously published data are not found. The most common methods of primary research are interviews, surveys, and observation.

- **(LO 12-3) Discuss intellectual property.**
  Intellectual property is something that comes from a person's mind, such as an idea, an invention, or a process. Intellectual property laws protect a person's or a company's inventions, artistic works, and other intellectual property.

- **(LO 12-4) Explain how to credit sources used in a formal paper.**
  This is done by summarizing the work in your own words or by directly quoting part of it. If your paper includes information from sources you have researched, these sources should be acknowledged. A citation lists the author, title, and publisher of the source; date of publication; and location of the publisher or online address. Citations can be listed in footnotes on the pages where the references occur or in a bibliography or works cited/reference at the end of the paper.

GLOSSARY TERMS

Visit the G-W Learning companion website at **www.g-wlearning.com/careereducation/** to review the following glossary terms.

research	representative sampling
data	intellectual property
qualitative data	piracy
quantitative data	copyright
secondary research	infringement
primary research	public domain
focus group	citation
survey	

REVIEW

1. Differentiate between informal and formal papers.

2. Summarize secondary research.

3. How can the credibility of a secondary research source be evaluated?

4. Summarize primary research.

5. Describe two types of interviews that can be conducted.

6. What is needed to make observations successful?

7. Discuss intellectual property.

8. What do copyright laws protect?

9. How does material become part of public domain?

10. Identify information needed to credit a source for a formal paper.

CRITICAL THINKING

1. Identify examples of times you have conducted secondary research. Describe where you found your sources, such as a textbook or online source, and how you confirmed the credibility of each.

2. The most common methods of primary research for a paper are interviews, surveys, and observation. If you were assigned a research paper that required primary research, on what criteria would you base your choice of research method?

3. Which writing reference book do you use to guide you when you are writing a paper or citing material in the footnotes or at the end of the paper? Why did you choose that specific resource?

4. When performing research online, it is easy to cut and paste information into a document with the intention to rephrase and cite sources at a later date. However, this can lead to unintentional plagiarism. Discuss how this situation can be avoided.

5. Photocopying copyrighted material is illegal and unethical. What is your opinion of a friend photocopying a textbook chapter instead of buying the textbook?

INTERNET ACTIVITY

Digital Citizenship. Digital citizenship is the standard of appropriate behavior when using technology. Using the Internet, perform secondary research on *digital citizenship*. Summarize how it influences your responsibility as a student.

Effective Surveys. Using the Internet, conduct a search for the phrase *how to write effective survey questions*. Research types of questions that are the most effective for gathering data. What question writing tips did you find?

SKILLS PRACTICE

Visit the G-W Learning companion website at **www.g-wlearning.com/careereducation/** to access and complete the following study skills practice activity:

Study Skills Activity 12-1 Crediting Sources. When referencing other people's work in a paper, it is important to give proper credit to the original work by placing it in a citation. Open the 12-1 file and write citations that could be used for a paper.

CHAPTER 13

Writing a College Paper

WAYHOME studio/Shutterstock.com

BEFORE YOU READ

Before you begin reading this chapter, see what you already know about writing a college paper by taking a pretest. The pretest is available at **www.g-wlearning.com/careereducation/**

LEARNING OUTCOMES

On completion of this chapter, prepare to:

13-1 Identify steps to take when preparing to write a research paper.

13-2 Summarize options for approach and outline when presenting information in a research paper.

13-3 Describe common parts of a formal paper.

13-4 Describe common parts of an informal paper.

13-5 List actions to take when formatting a paper.

Preparing to Write

During your academic career, you will be required to write various papers such as a research paper. A **research paper** is a formal report that involves extensive research, critical thinking, and analysis of a position taken by the writer.

The assignment will typically begin with your instructor noting a due date for the paper. Time management is important if you are to research, write, and submit the paper on time. Break the writing tasks into multiple goals, and assign a target date for each goal on your calendar. Start by noting the date the paper is due. Back up that date by at least a week, and record it on your calendar as your target date for completion. This will give you some breathing room at the end of the writing process to polish your finished paper. How many weeks do you think it will take you to research and write the paper? Work backwards and commit dates for each task. Allow extra time for unexpected events.

There are steps that you will take as you prepare to write a research paper. These steps include understanding the type of paper, topic, audience, and conducting the research as shown in Figure 13-1.

A research paper assignment typically begins with the instructor assigning a due date.

goodluz/Shutterstock.com

Decide Type of Paper

The goal of a research paper is to share your ideas about a topic and support your findings with evidence. There are two common types of research papers.

- *Analytical papers* include both information and analysis of the data. These papers often provide conclusions or recommendations drawn from the analysis.

- *Argumentative papers* typically present sides of an issue by presenting facts. The writer might assume a side.

Select the Topic

The first step in writing a paper is to understand the focus of the paper. The instructor may assign a topic or have a list of topics from which to choose. Alternatively, you may be required to select a topic of your choosing. In this situation, start with a subject area and then narrow it to a specific topic.

After you select the topic, it is necessary to consider the proper scope of the content for the paper. The *scope* is the guideline of how much information to include. Is the paper going to be detailed or general? Which key points will be included? The scope includes the boundaries within which you should keep your writing.

Identify the Audience

Identifying the audience will help you make decisions about the approach, style, tone, and level of formality of the paper. The first question to ask is if the audience is an instructor, a committee, the class, or other parties. Answering this question

Figure 13-1 Follow these steps when working on a research paper.

Writing a Research Paper

Choose a topic ▸ Perform research ▸ Create an outline ▸ Write first draft ▸ Revise paper ▸ Finalize paper

Goodheart-Willcox Publisher

helps to determine the depth of information the audience already possesses about the topic. The audience might have prior knowledge or biases that you need to consider. You might need to provide background information, vocabulary definitions, and other data in the paper. Knowing this information can help you determine the stance you should take on a topic, especially when presenting an argumentative or analytical paper. In addition, reviewing the demographics can help note preferences for language and style.

Perform Research

In Chapter 12, you learned how to conduct secondary and primary research. Collecting data is an important step in preparing to write a paper.

After you have collected the data, analyze your findings. What did you learn? How can you use the information to convey your ideas in the paper? First, you must be able to draw conclusions about your findings. Then, you can make a recommendation based on what you have learned.

Presenting the Information

Once your research is finished and your sources are organized, you are ready to determine how the information will be presented. You must first decide the approach you will be taking and then outline the order of the material.

Approach

Formal papers are written in the third person. Ask your instructor if there are any other standards that must be followed, such as the formatting style.

As you prepare to write, select an approach that will support your material. You must choose the direct or indirect approach in order to achieve the desired outcome. The *direct approach* is desirable when the reader is expecting a straightforward message. When using the direct approach, start with a general statement of purpose followed by supporting details. When using the *indirect approach*, discuss supporting details upfront. This prepares the reader for your general statement of purpose or conclusions.

Asking for feedback and suggestions from friends can help a final paper be more effective.

Jacob Lund/Shutterstock.com

Outline

After you have decided the approach, the next step is to create an outline. Think ahead, and note the main points you want to cover. Once you have all the information, arrange it in the order that will make the paper most effective. You can choose to organize the paper by chronological or sequential order, order of importance, cause-and-effect order, or problem-solution order. To accomplish your goal, you can use a combination of two or more of these approaches as well.

- *Chronological or sequential order.* When you are reporting events or discussing a process, the chronological or sequential order is a good choice. *Chronological* means in order of time. *Sequential* means in order of sequence. In chronological or sequential order, start with the earliest events and proceed to the most recent. A variation is to use the reverse order in which you present the most recent events first.

- *Order of importance.* When organizing by order of importance, present information from most to least important. Readers can easily follow this logic. In some cases, it is better to present information in the reverse order, from least to most important.

- *Cause-and-effect order.* This order is useful when your paper reflects an investigation. This approach lists facts or ideas followed by conclusions. You should report your opinions only after careful research and fact-finding.

- *Problem-solution order.* This organization type works well when the paper describes a problem and offers a solution or multiple solutions. By presenting the problem, you communicate to the reader why an action is needed. Give the reader options for solving the problem.

After creating an outline, complete the first draft, and revise the paper as many times as necessary to create the final product. Focus on constructing the content and editing the document until it is in finished form.

Parts of a Formal Paper

The parts of a formal paper, such as a research paper, vary according to the purpose of the paper and the topic. Several common parts can appear in a formal paper. These include a title page, a table of contents, an introduction, a body, conclusions and recommendations, and citations.

Title Page

All formal papers should have a title page designed for readability and visual appeal. These elements belong on the title page:

- name of the paper
- name of the class
- your name
- date the paper is submitted

Include any additional information, such as the college or instructor's name, on the title page as noted by your instructor.

Table of Contents

A table of contents is necessary so the reader knows what is included in the paper. The **table of contents** lists the major sections and subsections within the paper with page numbers. This page can be referred to as the *table of contents* or *contents*.

Introduction

The reader's attention should be captured by an overview of the content of the paper. An introduction usually discusses the purpose of the paper and the benefits of the ideas or recommendations you are presenting. It often covers the following information.

- The history or background leading to the preparation of the paper.
- The purpose for which the paper was written, including the need or justification for the paper.
- The scope of the paper, including what is covered and, if necessary, what is not covered.
- Definitions of terms that might present problems for certain readers.
- The method of gathering information, facts, and figures for the paper.

Body

The body of the paper contains all the information, data, and statistics you assemble. Providing supporting facts and figures from reliable sources will help the audience understand the content. Your outline will help you organize ideas and information in a logical manner. When writing the body, consider the tone of the paper, potential biases the audience may have, the audience's level of knowledge, and the readability level.

Tone

When writing your paper, be aware of the tone that you have chosen to use. **Tone** is an impression of the overall content of the message. If the topic you are writing about is very high level, a formal tone is more likely to achieve this goal. You want to convince the reader you have thoroughly studied the topic and your facts and figures are highly trustworthy. If, on the other hand, you are writing a paper on student activities that boost school spirit, a conversational tone is appropriate. This friendlier tone will help set the stage for the theme of the paper.

Bias

Sometimes, bias on the part of the reader influences your handling of the topic. Consider biases the reader might bring to the subject matter and develop content to address them. Avoid generalizations, stereotypes, and making statements based on personal experience rather than on facts.

Knowledge

Assess the level of knowledge the audience has and if there is variation within the audience. The amount of background information given and the need to define terms depend on your assessment of the audience's prior knowledge. The higher the reader knowledge is in the topic of the paper, the less explanation is needed.

Readability

Another aspect to keep in mind while preparing the body of your paper is readability. **Readability** is a measure of how easy it is for the audience to understand your writing. It also measures how easy it is for the audience to locate information within your paper.

Conclusions and Recommendations

Your closing should summarize the key points of your paper. In some cases, you will want to close with conclusions and recommendations based on your study or analysis. **Conclusions** are the writer's summary of what the audience should take away from the paper. **Recommendations** are actions the writer believes the reader should take. Both of these should follow logically from the information presented in the body of the paper. If you make a leap in logic, you risk losing credibility with the audience.

Collecting data is an important step in writing a research paper.

ESB Professional/Shutterstock.com

Citations

You need to acknowledge the sources you have researched, if your paper contains information from them. You must credit all sources used for a paper as illustrated in Chapter 12. The citation style varies depending on the style you have been told to use by your instructor. Be sure to follow the style directions exactly in order to prevent claims of plagiarism.

Optional Elements

Complex papers might contain other elements. These other elements help the reader find information and understand the contents.

- *List of visuals.* A paper can be enhanced greatly with the use of visuals in the forms of tables and figures. If visuals are used, include a list at the front of the paper with page references. This aids readers in quickly finding information.

- *Glossary.* If terminology used in the paper might be unfamiliar to some readers, include a list at the end of the paper to define important terms.

- *Appendices.* Information users might want to refer to, but not integral to the body of the paper, might be included at the back of the paper in an appendix. For example, if your paper includes survey results, you might provide the survey questionnaire in an appendix.

These optional elements are opportunities to include extra information that might not fit into the scope of the paper's body.

Parts of an Informal Paper

In addition to formal research papers, you will be assigned informal papers such as a book report. A book report is an *informational paper* which includes facts, data, or other types of information. These papers do not attempt to analyze the data or persuade the reader. They take a neutral position and simply explain a topic.

An informal paper does not require the research that a formal paper requires. This type of paper generally uses a casual tone and personal pronouns. An informal paper does not have a table of contents, appendices, or other common components of a formal paper. Typically, it has an introduction, a body, and a conclusion and is only a few pages long. If you are writing a book report or other informational papers, the instructor will convey the format that it should take.

Introduction

The introduction states the purpose of the paper. This is typically where the rest of the paper is briefly summarized.

Body

The body contains the information of the paper. Decide whether the content has subtopics that will help the reader skim and scan for information. For example, a short paper on a site visit to view a campus might be divided into these sections: Location, Campus Description, and Cost. The body of the paper should be of sufficient length to communicate the purpose of the document.

Conclusion

Papers should end with a brief summary of the main points from the writer's point of view. If you use headings, this section might be labeled *Conclusion*, *Recommendations*, or *Summary*. The conclusion is the last paragraph, if your paper does not have headings. In the above example, the writer would likely conclude with a recommendation about whether to attend the campus.

Formatting a Paper

The final step of the writing process is to format the pages carefully so the paper appears polished and professional. Depending on if the paper is formal or informal, your instructor will probably provide formatting guidelines. Alternatively, you can use templates provided in Microsoft Word or other word-processing software.

When a topic covers more than one key point or important issue, consider using headings as a design element, if consistent with the style guidelines you were given by your instructor. **Headings** are words and phrases introducing sections of text. They are leveled, beginning with the section-opener title and continuing with the main headings and subheadings. Headings organize blocks of information in a document and serve as guideposts to alert the reader to what is coming. Most narrative text can be divided into main topics and subtopics with no more than three levels of headings.

The use of white space for readability is important. White space includes margins, space between paragraphs, and other blank space on the page. Style manuals such as *The Chicago Manual of Style*, the Modern Language Association's *MLA Handbook*, and the *Publication Manual of the American Psychological Association* include formatting guidelines.

The writing process also includes soliciting feedback. If there is someone available to read your paper, have this person give it a final review. Consider asking a friend or visiting a campus writing or tutoring center. Ask for feedback and suggestions that will make the paper more effective.

Proofread the paper one final time. Correct any grammar, spelling, or formatting mistakes. Errors distract from the message and suggest you were careless in preparing the communication. Your written work will be judged on its correctness and appearance.

Angeles College
440 Wilshire Blvd., Suite 310
Los Angeles, CA 90010
Tel. (213) 487-2211

SUMMARY

- **(LO 13-1) Identify steps to take when preparing to write a research paper.**
  The steps to take when writing a paper include identifying the type of paper, selecting a topic, identifying the audience, and conducting the research.
- **(LO 13-2) Summarize options for approach and outline when presenting information in a research paper.**
  As you prepare to write, select an approach that will support your material. You must choose the direct or indirect approach. Arrange your information in the order that will make the paper most effective. You can choose to organize by chronological or sequential order, order of importance, cause-and-effect order, or problem-solution order.
- **(LO 13-3) Describe common parts of a formal paper.**
  The common parts of a formal paper are the title page, table of contents, introduction, body, conclusions and recommendations, and citations. List of visuals, a glossary, or appendices are additional parts that can be included for a complex paper.
- **(LO 13-4) Describe common parts of an informal paper.**
  The common parts of an informal paper are the introduction, body, and conclusion.
- **(LO 13-5) List actions to take when formatting a paper.**
  The final step of the writing process is to format the pages carefully so the paper appears polished and professional. Format the headings, format the white space, include margins and paragraph spacing, solicit feedback, and proofread the paper a final time.

GLOSSARY TERMS

Visit the G-W Learning companion website at **www.g-wlearning.com/careereducation/** to review the following glossary terms.

research paper	conclusion
table of contents	recommendation
tone	heading
readability	

REVIEW

1. What are the steps to take to prepare to write a research paper?

2. List examples of common types of research papers.

3. Summarize two common approaches taken when writing a paper.

4. Explain four outlining strategies for a paper.

5. Describe common parts of a formal paper.

6. Why is it important to assess the level of knowledge the audience has on the topic of your paper?

7. What does readability measure?

8. What are some optional elements that enhance the understanding of a paper?

9. Describe parts of an informal paper.

10. List actions to take when formatting a paper.

CRITICAL THINKING

1. Identify the steps you take when preparing to write a paper. How do you decide the topic, the audience, and where to begin research?

2. What type of outline strategy to you typically use when writing a paper—chronological or sequential order, order of importance, cause-and-effect order, or problem-solution order? Why is it your favorite?

3. Which approach do you prefer to use when writing—direct or indirect? Why is that your preference?

4. Which type of paper do you prefer to write—informational, analytical, or argumentative? Why did you choose that type?

5. Tone of writing can win an audience or lose it. Describe the tone of your writing that you usually use for your papers.

INTERNET ACTIVITY

Avoiding Biases. When writing a paper, you can lose credibility with your audience if you show bias in your facts or analysis. Using the Internet, research *how to avoid bias in writing*. What did you learn from your research?

Online Writing Lab. Most educational institutions have an online writing lab that offers service to students to help in their academic assignments. Conduct an Internet search for *online writing lab* or visit your own school's website. Select one area of the website that could provide you the most value in your academic writing. Summarize the advantages that it offers.

SKILLS PRACTICE

Visit the G-W Learning companion website at **www.g-wlearning.com/careereducation/** to access and complete the following study skills practice activity:

Study Skills Activity 13-1 Improving Your Formatting Skills. Formatting a paper is an important final step in the writing process. Proper formatting makes the final document appear polished and professional. Open the 13-1 file. Edit the document and format it to create a professional appearance.

Rachaphak /Shutterstock.com

BEFORE YOU READ

Before you begin reading this chapter, see what you already know about stress management by taking a pretest. The pretest is available at **www.g-wlearning.com/careereducation/**

LEARNING OUTCOMES

On completion of this chapter, prepare to:

14-1 Define stress-management skills.

14-2 Cite ways to focus on self-health.

14-3 List examples of relaxation techniques.

14-4 Identify sources of help to manage stress.

Stress-Management Skills

Being a student is not an easy job. Most students juggle classes with work and other responsibilities. It can be overwhelming at times. All the responsibilities, expectations, and activities existing in students' personal and school lives can create a great deal of anxiety and pressure.

Stress-management skills are the skills that enable an individual to identify and control stress. **Stress** is the body's reaction to increased demands or dangerous situations. It can manifest itself in many ways including nervousness, anger, feelings of being overwhelmed, frequent headaches, upset stomach, or even high blood pressure. Stress can be caused by *external triggers* such as receiving a low grade on a paper or by *internal triggers* such as putting too much pressure on yourself to be successful. **Stress management** is a variety of strategies used to cope with stress and limit its effects. Figure 14-1 identifies some common stress-management strategies.

A certain amount of stress can be positive at times. Some people are driven to perform when pressured to meet a deadline. Others react to the release of adrenaline that stress triggers, which speeds up the heart and increases metabolism for endurance. The goal is to identify positive stress, as well as negative stress, in your life. When stress becomes negative, it is time to evaluate and get help, if needed.

Stress can be caused by external triggers such as trying to keep up with class assignments.

Africa Studio /Shutterstock.com

Focus on Self-Health

Stressful times often cause people to lose sight of their physical, mental, and emotional needs. It is increasingly important for you to be in touch with your needs when under tremendous amounts of stress. Lack of care can increase the risk of illness.

Figure 14-1 Stress management is a variety of strategies used to cope with stress and limit its effects.

Stress-Management Strategies	
Identify stress triggers	• Identify where you were when you started feeling stressed. • Recall the activity in which you were engaged. • Remember if there was a particular situation or conversation involved. • Recognize if other people were around that may have contributed to your stress.
Attend to physical needs	• Get an adequate amount of sleep. • Eat regular and healthy meals. • Avoid foods providing a quick jolt of energy, such as sugar and caffeine. • Schedule regular exercise.
Practice time management	• Schedule tasks and commitments for the day. • Plan time for breaks and meals.
Be proactive, not reactive	• Focus on the positive. • Deal with the challenge rather than worry. • Set realistic goals. • Find balance in your personal, school, and work lives.

Goodheart-Willcox Publisher

It is not possible to avoid all stress in life, so it is important to learn how to manage it in a healthy way. Avoiding substance abuse, getting more sleep, getting regular exercise, and practicing good eating habits are imperative to living a healthy, stress-controlled lifestyle. Practicing these habits will help keep you healthy and better able to handle any stressful situations that come your way.

Avoid Substance Abuse

Stress is often a leading reason why people become involved in substance abuse. They think abusing a substance will help them feel better. This behavior, however, often results in the opposite happening. Not only does prolonged substance abuse ultimately result in feelings of depression, it can also lead to adverse health issues. Additionally, extended use can lead to social, academic, professional, and legal problems.

Get More Sleep

A lack of regular sleep can increase a person's stress level. On average, eight to ten hours of sleep is recommended. The inability to sleep prevents the brain from "powering down" and can result in an increase in stress levels and a decrease in health. If you are having difficulty getting sleep, consider the following suggestions to remedy the situation.

- Avoid use of digital devices for at least 30 minutes before bed.
- Opt to use relaxation techniques before turning to medication.
- Take a warm shower before going to bed.
- Read a book or magazine to unwind.
- Go to bed the same time each evening.

Get More Exercise

Exercise is an easy way to reduce stress. Physical activity releases *endorphins*, which are chemicals found in the brain that affect emotions. The release of endorphins can reduce the effects of stress on your body as well as lower your heart rate and blood pressure. At times, prolonged aerobic exercise can actually evoke a feeling of *euphoria*, a feeling of intense excitement or happiness, and decrease sensitivity to pain. Let off steam by walking, running, bicycling, swimming, working out, or playing a sport.

Practice Good Eating Habits

For some people, eating is a source of stress relief. If you eat when you are stressed, it is important to avoid junk food and choose something nutritious instead. Eat fruits and vegetables to satisfy hunger cravings and drink water instead of drinks with caffeine, carbonated drinks, and sugar.

Practice good eating habits. Avoid skipping meals, and instead, make it a point to sit down at a table and eat balanced meals during the day. In addition, pack healthy snacks, such as granola bars, in your bag to help calm hunger in between meals.

Relaxation Techniques

A good way to reduce stress is to relax. People under tremendous amounts of stress often have trouble relaxing. It is important to reserve some time for total relaxation. When you are relaxed, you feel at peace with yourself and the rest of the world. You feel renewed and regain strength.

If you begin to feel stressed, you might need to take time to relax and have fun. Relaxing helps slow down your pace and lessen stress. Figure 14-2 suggests ways to positively manage stress and help control its effects.

Some additional examples of relaxation techniques are deep breathing, progressive muscle relaxation, meditation, and having a positive attitude.

Deep Breathing

The mechanics of taking slow, deep breaths help calm the body and mind. Sit up straight and slowly inhale through your nose. Let your abdomen expand and feel the breath fill you. Start in your core and let the air work its way to the top of your head. Gradually exhale through your mouth and let all your air come out in the reverse order. Repeat the process for a few breaths. Deep breathing is not only good for reducing stress and relieving built-up tension, but it can also lower blood pressure and reduce your heart rate.

Progressive Muscle Relaxation

Progressive muscle relaxation is exactly what it sounds like—the relaxation of different muscle groups over a short period of time. This is accomplished through tensing a group of muscles when inhaling and relaxing them when exhaling. This can also be achieved by tensing all the muscles in your body, and then, starting with your feet, relaxing each muscle group until you have become completely relaxed. You can perform this while sitting in a comfortable chair or lying down. Progressive muscle relaxation is an excellent tool for reducing anxiety, stress, and overall body tension as well as for those who have difficulty falling asleep.

Meditation

Meditation is the practice of focusing one's mind for a period of time as a method of relaxation or for religious purposes. A few minutes of meditation each day can help ease anxiety and stress.

Many people have a preconceived notion of meditation, but in reality, meditation is what each person makes it. For example, you can meditate by finding a quiet area of your house or campus and sitting idle for 15-to-30 minutes a day.

The key to meditation is to allow your mind to relax. This can be accomplished easily by focusing on your breathing patterns. Often, counting each breath you take can help clear your mind and help you feel refreshed and energized by the end of your session.

Some people find it helpful to have guidance when they first start the practice of meditation. There are numerous apps available for walking beginners through varying techniques.

Figure 14-2 Relaxation techniques can help decrease stress levels.

Relaxation Techniques

- Learn to laugh more.
- Spend time with a pet, family member, or friend.
- Take a nap.
- Do something nice for someone else.
- Limit Internet or cell phone time.
- Keep things in perspective.
- Read something inspiring, entertaining, or informative.
- See a movie, play, concert, or television program.
- Attend a lecture or social function.

Goodheart-Willcox Publisher

Positive Attitude

Stress can sometimes be reduced through optimism. Reassessing how you perceive negative aspects of life can reduce stress. By focusing on the positive, you decrease the stress associated with the negative. Find friends who have a positive attitude and refrain from offering negative reinforcement. **Negative reinforcement** occurs when you talk with someone who encourages your negative attitudes.

Use positive self-talk and take a few minutes at the beginning of every day to tell yourself about good things in your life. Starting your day with positive self-talk can increase the likelihood that you will have a good day.

A lack of regular sleep can increase a person's stress level.

Fotos593/Shutterstock.com

Seek Help

When you feel your level of stress rising, it is a good idea to seek the advice of a person who is not involved in the situation. Talking with someone you trust can provide insight into your situation. Sometimes, just the act of talking is reassuring and relieves stress. A friend or family member might be able to give suggestions about ways to handle the situation. He or she might help you see things more clearly or from a different view.

If you need professional help, reach out to someone who is trained to diagnose mental health problems and help those who struggle with emotional control. Types of mental health professionals include psychologists, therapists, and counselors. Most college campuses will have a wellness center with free therapists who can help you talk through your problems. If you cannot see a mental health professional face-to-face, consider calling a free therapy hotline for help to handle stress.

If talking does not help, try writing about your situation in a journal. Write about problems and how they make you feel. Do not focus on grammar, spelling, or punctuation. Simply write out what comes to your mind. Putting your feelings in writing can help you analyze them. Are your feelings justified, or are you being overly sensitive? Are you taking responsibility for your role in the situation, or are you blaming others? You can also write about several ways to resolve the situation. Seeing the options written out might help you make a good choice for dealing with the stressful situation.

SUMMARY

- **(LO 14-1) Define stress-management skills.**
  Stress-management skills are the skills that enable an individual to identify and control stress. Stress is the body's reaction to increased demands or dangerous situations caused by external or internal triggers.
- **(LO 14-2) Cite ways to focus on self-health.**
  Ways to focus on self-health include avoiding substance abuse, getting more sleep, getting more exercise, and practicing good eating habits.
- **(LO 14-3) List examples of relaxation techniques.**
  Some examples of relaxation techniques are deep breathing, progressive muscle relaxation, meditation, and having a positive attitude.
- **(LO 14-4) Identify sources of help to manage stress.**
  Talking with someone you trust can give insight into your situation. Your friend or family member might be able to give you suggestions about ways to handle your situation. If you need professional help, reach out to someone who is trained to diagnose mental health problems and those who struggle with emotional control. If talking does not help, try writing about your situation in a journal.

GLOSSARY TERMS

Visit the G-W Learning companion website at **www.g-wlearning.com/careereducation/** to review the following glossary terms.

stress-management skills	progressive muscle relaxation
stress	meditation
stress management	negative reinforcement

REVIEW

1. What are stress-management skills?

2. Compare and contrast external and internal triggers.

3. Cite ways to focus on self-health.

4. What can a person do to help get more sleep?

5. What does the release of endorphins reduce?

6. List examples of relaxation techniques.

7. What is the difference between progressive muscle relaxation and meditation?

8. What happens when a person maintains a positive attitude?

9. Identify sources of help to manage stress.

10. How does writing in a journal help a person manage stress?

CRITICAL THINKING

1. Identify a stress-management skill in which you are proficient. Explain why you think you are proficient in this specific skill.

2. Describe how your sleeping and eating habits influence your health and stress level. What can you do to improve them?

3. What are some external sources of stress that you have experienced lately? How can you learn to manage these stressors?

4. What are some internal sources of stress that you have experienced lately? How can you learn to manage these stressors?

5. Identify someone in your life who you could talk to if you are feeling stressed. Why did you choose this person?

INTERNET ACTIVITY

Journaling for Stress Management. One technique to help manage stress is to keep a journal. Conduct research on how to *reduce stress by journaling.* Read about the benefits of writing down thoughts to put things in perspective. Summarize what you have learned and how you could use this technique to help manage stress.

Hotline Help. Sometimes stress can get beyond what personal techniques can reduce. In those cases, calling a free therapy hotline can be the best option. Conduct a search on *free therapy hotlines.* Find several that deal with different aspects of stress. Compare their pros and cons and summarize what you found.

SKILLS PRACTICE

Visit the G-W Learning companion website at **www.g-wlearning.com/careereducation/** to access and complete the following study skills practice activities:

Study Skills Activity 14-1 Stress Evaluation. To effectively manage stress, sources of stress must be identified and the effects of stress must be recognized. Open the 14-1 file and evaluate your current level of stress.

Study Skills Activity 14-2 Handling Stress. Everyone experiences stress at some point, and the best way to handle stress varies with the situation. Open the 14-2 file and read each reaction to stress. If the reaction is positive, place a check in the positive column. If the reaction is negative, place a check in the negative column.

APPENDIX A

Portfolio Development

Portfolio Development activities provide guidance for creating a personal portfolio to use when exploring volunteer, education and training, and career opportunities. This process requires that you self-reflect on personal accomplishments and skills as you create documentation for final presentation. Completing these activities will help you prepare a professional product for the job-application process, giving you a head start on your career search in an increasingly competitive workforce.

Lesson 1: Overview

When applying for a job, a volunteer position, or entry into an educational institution, one way to demonstrate your qualifications is to present a portfolio to the interviewer. A *portfolio* is a selection of related materials that you collect and organize to demonstrate your job qualifications, skills, and talents. For example, a certification showing you have completed Microsoft Office Specialist training could help you get a job at a local newspaper. A portfolio is a *dynamic document*, which means it should be reviewed and updated on a regular basis.

Visual artists and communication professionals have historically presented portfolios of their creative work when seeking jobs or admission to educational institutions. However, portfolios are now used in many professions. It is helpful to research and identify which type is appropriate for the industry in which you are applying for a position.

Commonly used formats for a portfolio are print and electronic. Job seekers will need copies of a print portfolio, as well as an electronic version, when applying for a position.

A *print portfolio* is a hard-copy version that can be carried to an interview. It can be presented in a three-ring binder with divider tabs or any other method that works for you.

An *electronic portfolio* is a digital version of a print portfolio. It can be saved to cloud-based storage services, flash drives, or CDs. There are many creative ways to present a digital portfolio. One option is to create an electronic presentation with slides for each item. Another option is to place the files on a CD. Websites also work well for presenting an electronic portfolio. The method you choose should allow the viewer to navigate and find items easily.

As you collect materials for your portfolio, you will need an effective strategy to keep the items clean, safe, and organized for assembly at the appropriate time. Structure and organization are important when working on an on-going project that includes multiple pieces. Never include an original document in a portfolio. Photocopy each document that you want to include and file the original in a safe place for future reference.

A large manila envelope works well to keep hard copies of documents, photos, awards, and other items safe. File folders also work well.

1. Research *Types of Portfolios* and select the one that is most appropriate for you and your career goals.

2. Consider and plan for the technology that might be needed for creating and scanning documents for an electronic portfolio. You may need access to desktop-publishing software, scanners, cameras, and other digital equipment or software.

3. Create a master spreadsheet to track each component that you add to your portfolio. Save the spreadsheet as MASTER_PORTFOLIO with your last name, for example MASTER_PORTFOLIO_SMITH, or use a different naming convention that is suitable for your management system. Ask your instructor where you should save your file. It is recommended to use a flash drive as a backup, in addition to the school network, so that you have access to your information at all times.

4. Decide on a management system that works for you as you collect items. You may list each document alphabetically, by category, date, or other convention that helps you keep track of each document you are including. For each activity you complete, remember to update the spreadsheet.

Lesson 2: Objective

Before you begin collecting information, it will be beneficial to write an objective for your portfolio. An *objective* is one or two complete sentences that state what you want to accomplish. Your objective will help keep you on track as you build your portfolio.

First, focus on your short-term and long-term goals. A *short-term goal* is a goal you would like to achieve in the next one to two years. A *long-term goal* is a goal you wish to accomplish in the next five to ten years. Your objective should be written in a way that allows you to achieve these goals. For example, if your short-term goal is to find employment within a year, but your long-term goal is to work in a field more closely related to your career goal, your objective could be: "I will be actively employed within a year and will be working in my desired field within five years." By focusing on your goals, you will be able to write a descriptive objective for your portfolio.

When writing your objective, include enough details so you can easily judge when it is accomplished. Consider this objective: "I will try to get into graduate school." Such an objective is too general. A better, more detailed objective might read: "I will get accepted into the graduate program at one of my top-three colleges of choice." Creating a clear objective is a good starting point for beginning to work on your portfolio.

1. Using word-processing software, create a document with the heading "Portfolio Objective." Then create two subheadings, one that says "Short-Term Goals" and another that says "Long-Term Goals." List your goals under their respective heading. These are the goals on which you should focus when writing your objective.

2. Next, write your portfolio objective based on those goals. Keep in mind that this objective will likely change as your ideas and goals evolve during the portfolio creation process.

3. Save this document as PORTFOLIO_OBJECTIVE with your last name, for example PORTFOLIO_OBJECTIVE_SMITH, or use a different naming convention that is suitable for the management system you put into place in Lesson 1. Remember to back up your documents on a flash drive.

4. Place this document as the first page of your portfolio to guide you as you build it. This is your working document, so remember to remove it when you organize the final product.

5. This is your first activity, so record it on the master portfolio spreadsheet you created in the last lesson. Title your first entry Portfolio Objective.

Lesson 3: References and Recommendations

A *reference* is a person who is ready and willing to recommend an individual and answer questions about that person's qualifications and background. It is a person who knows your skills, talents, or personal traits and is willing to recommend you for a job, community service position, or perhaps entrance into a college program.

References can include your instructors, a manager at your part-time job, or counselors who know about your skills and interests. Someone you know from your personal life, such as a youth-group leader, can also be listed. However, you should *not* list relatives. Consider which references can best recommend you for the position for which you are applying and always get permission from the person before using his or her name.

A *letter of recommendation* is a letter in which your qualities and abilities to perform in a specific capacity are assessed by a person you know well. It highlights your achievements in your academic or professional career and is usually written by an instructor, supervisor, or someone else who is familiar with your qualifications for a given job or application. The purpose of the letter is to advocate for you as a candidate for a position. A letter of recommendation will probably be written by a person who also agrees to serve as a reference for you. Two or three letters of recommendation are sufficient.

1. Ask several people who know you well if they are willing to serve as a reference for you. Using word-processing software, create a document that includes the names and contact information for those individuals. Each entry should include complete contact information for the person. Use the heading "Personal References" and your name. This page should follow your résumé when you are organizing your portfolio for presentation. Save this file as PERSONAL_REFERENCES with your last name, for example PERSONAL_REFERENCES_SMITH, or use a different naming convention that is suitable for the management system you implemented in Lesson 1. Back up the file on your flash drive.

2. Contact several people from your references and ask if they are willing to write a letter of recommendation for you. For those contacts who agree to write letters, suggest to them a date by which you would like to receive it. Writing the letter can, and should, take some time, so plan in advance. When organizing your portfolio, it is suggested that these letters follow your personal references document.

3. Record the creation of your Personal References document on your master portfolio spreadsheet. In addition, record each person you contacted for a reference.

Lesson 4: Testimonials

A *testimonial* is a formal statement from a customer or other professional that certifies a person's qualifications or character. Generally briefer than a letter of recommendation, a testimonial focuses on a specific action a person executed that was exceptional in nature. The person writing the testimonial may not know you personally, but is validating the work or service you provided.

For example, if you work at a computer store and help a customer set up a computer, the customer may be very happy with your work. That customer may contact your supervisor through an e-mail with a testimonial that says, "Justin was an outstanding technical support person. He was patient, set up my computer, and helped me get started. I want to convey my appreciation for his help." Similar to letters of recommendation, testimonials validate claims of abilities that you include in your résumé and portfolio. If your employer forwards any positive written customer comments about you, save these for inclusion in your portfolio.

You may also have testimonials from instructors who made complimentary remarks on a paper you wrote or a project in which you participated. A former employer may have sent you an e-mail with congratulations on a personal accomplishment of yours. These are all testimonials that validate your abilities.

Have you been the subject of a newspaper article that summarizes a contribution, service, or personal accomplishment? This, too, is a testimonial of your skills and talents. Include newspaper articles in which you are the subject.

You can also include employer evaluations in your portfolio. Evaluations serve as a snapshot of your performance as an employee. They reflect your work habits, strengths, and contributions to an employer. If you decide to include an evaluation, be selective in the one you choose.

1. Sort through testimonials you have collected. Include assignments that have an instructor's written comments about your work. Print any e-mails from community members or other professionals who complimented your actions on something you did for that person. Attach notes to each document to identify (1) what it is and (2) why it is included in the portfolio. For example, a note on a research paper you wrote might say, "Research paper, Professor Dansby commenting on my writing skills." Be sure to update your master portfolio spreadsheet as you add testimonials to your portfolio.

2. If you have any evaluations from supervisors of any jobs you may have, review and decide if these would be appropriate to include.

Lesson 5: Transcripts

A *transcript* is an official academic record of the courses a student has completed, the school where the courses were taken, grades received, dates the courses were taken, and a cumulative grade point average (GPA). Including a transcript as part of your portfolio provides evidence of your scholastic achievements. Transcripts reflect academic successes and confirm the candidate's statements that courses of study have indeed been completed as indicated on a résumé. Employers may ask for a transcript at some point in the interviewing process. By including a copy in your portfolio, it shows organization and anticipation on the part of the candidate, which are signs of leadership.

When you contact your school for a copy of your transcript, you will likely be asked if you want an unofficial or official copy. An unofficial copy can generally be received by a student at no cost. For an official transcript, there may be a small fee requested. However, some schools may not release official transcripts to students. Each school has different guidelines regarding transcripts, so check with your advisor regarding transcript policies.

1. Determine if you should request an unofficial or official transcript.

2. Contact and obtain transcripts from your school. This may require a wait time, so plan accordingly.

3. Add dates for when you requested and received your transcript to your master portfolio spreadsheet.

Lesson 6: Certificates

A *certificate* is a document that serves as evidence of completion of an activity, training, or other accomplishment. For example, a certificate might show that you completed training or a class. Another one might show that you can key data at a certain speed.

Certificates are sometimes awarded to an individual as proof of receipt of scholarships, grants, or other recognition. For example, those who served in the military will probably have certificates that reflect awards, ranks, or other honors that were earned.

Diplomas are certificates and should be a part of a portfolio. Some certificates provide evidence of specialized training without a degree being granted. These programs are designed for individuals who are not seeking a degree, but are looking to update their current skills or taking courses specifically for employment.

Certification is a professional status earned by an individual after passing an exam focused on a specific body of knowledge. Some jobs *require* certification. For example, a position as an information technology specialist may require industry-specific hardware or software certifications. Already having and displaying a certification makes it more likely you will be seriously considered for the position.

1. Collect certificates of accomplishment that you have earned that are not associated with a degree or certification. You can arrange them in order of importance or dates earned.

2. Collect diplomas, proof of certification, and other examples that relate to educational accomplishments. These should also be arranged in a logical order.

3. Update your master portfolio spreadsheet.

Lesson 7: Clubs and Organizations

Participation in an organization, academic club, or sport demonstrates that you have the skill set to work with others and be a team player. Many soft skills, such as appreciation for diversity, leadership, and social responsibility, are learned from participating in a club or group. Documenting that you have been a member of an organization shows an employer that you are responsible, a hard worker, and a team player.

Networking skills can also be learned from interacting with club members and its leadership. *Networking* means talking with people and developing relationships that can lead to potential career opportunities.

Showing evidence that you have participated in competitive events is a valuable addition to a portfolio. These competitions support lifelong learning and the application of the skills learned in real-world situations. Participation in competitive events encourages leadership, teamwork, and career development. If you have participated in an event for a club or sports team, write a summary of your role and what you learned from the experience.

1. Identify organizations, academic clubs, or sports teams to which you belong. Create a document that lists each membership using word-processing software. Include the name of each organization, its contact information, and the dates that you were active. Use the heading "Clubs and Organizations," or another appropriate title, and your name. Save the document, and update your master portfolio spreadsheet. Remember to back up each document on your flash drive.

Lesson 8: Social Responsibility

Social responsibility is a cause that many businesses support and encourage from their employees. Workplace studies show that employees who are socially responsible are, by nature, generally ethical workers, loyal employees, and productive in their responsibilities.

Social responsibility can be demonstrated in many ways, and you can start with activities at your current job or school. For example, you may have organized a green team at your school to initiate a recycling program. Or, you may have participated in a campaign to "turn off the lights" and conserve energy for your employer. Documentation of these activities reflects social responsibility.

Participating in community service is an example of social responsibility. Evidence of community service can sometimes be criteria that employers use when vetting potential job candidates. Serving the community shows that a candidate is well rounded, socially aware, and capable of working well with others. For some individuals seeking a job, volunteer work could substitute for actual paid employment. Showing that you spent regular hours supporting a social cause is as valuable, in some situations, as paid work experience. By including evidence of community service or other socially responsible activities, a candidate can attract the attention of a person reviewing job applicants and move up on the list of potential interviewees.

If you have participated in an activity that reflects social responsibility, consider creating a video that informs viewers about it. Suppose you volunteer with a group that helps repair homes for elderly homeowners. The video could show scenes from the worksites and comments from the residents. Be sure you have permission to include other people in your video before doing so.

1. Using word-processing software, create a document that lists socially responsible projects in which you have taken part at school, work, or in your community. Use the heading "Service Projects," or something similar, along with your name. List the name of the programs, date(s) of service, and activities that you performed. If you received an award related to this service, mention it here.

2. Update your master portfolio spreadsheet to include your service projects. Back up your files on your flash drive.

Lesson 9: Writing Samples

Academic samples are important to include in a portfolio to show your accomplishments in school. You may want to start your collection with samples of your best writing. Writing skills are necessary for success in every part of life including academics and career. Therefore, it is important to demonstrate your ability to communicate ideas and information through the written word.

As you review documents, collect those that highlight your writing skills. Select items you have written, such as essays, stories, or poems. Each person is different in terms of writing styles. Some can be as unique as a fingerprint. Focus on selecting items that not only positively demonstrate your writing abilities but also provide a glimpse of your signature writing style.

1. Select writing examples that demonstrate your writing style. Be critical and choose your best creative writing sample, an article you have written for the school newspaper, or other documents of which you are proud.

2. For each document, attach a note that (1) describes what the sample is and (2) states why it is included in your portfolio. For example, a note on an article you wrote for the school newspaper might say, "Example of journalistic and investigative reporting skills."

3. Update your master portfolio spreadsheet to include your academic work samples.

Lesson 10: Skills and Talents

Employers, entrance committees, and neighborhood committees evaluate candidates based on their qualifications, including their skills and talents. For example, the ability to communicate effectively, adapt, and perform under pressure are qualities that employers seek in job applicants. These types of qualities are often called soft skills. *Soft skills* are applicable skills used to help an individual find a job, perform in the workplace, and gain success in any job or career. They are also called *employability skills* or *foundational skills*.

Employers also look for candidates who have the skills necessary to be successful in a position, such as the ability to use software programs or machinery. These abilities are called hard skills. *Hard skills* are measurable, observable, and critical skills necessary to perform required, work-related tasks of a position. They are also referred to as *job-specific skills*.

Do you have a special talent in an area such as art, music, or design? Some employers take interest in the talents of potential employees because it gives insight into who that person is. In addition, some talents rely on different methods of thought and information processing. For example, a musical talent requires a different type of thinking than rebuilding an engine does. Depending on the position for which you may be applying or interviewing, your talents may be criteria an employer uses to evaluate your qualifications.

Include samples of your skills or talents in your portfolio. Samples of documents can serve as evidence of your skills. However, talents may be challenging to prove. One way to document your talents is to create a video. For example, if you are an artist, create a video that shows your completed works. If you are a musician, create a video with segments from your performances. Be sure you have permission to include other people in your video before doing so.

Additionally, your portfolio should showcase the technical skills you have. Are you exceptionally good working with computers? Do you possess the skills that are needed for creating videos? Technical skills are very important for succeeding in school or at work.

Lesson 11: Foreign-Language Skills

Individuals who are fluent in a foreign language may, in some situations, have an advantage over other candidates in the job-search process or other competitive situations. As part of an interview with an organization, you may be asked about your ability to speak multiple languages or experience with people who speak a language other than your own. Many organizations are interested in this information for good reasons. They often serve people from a variety of geographic locations, cultures, and languages.

People who speak more than one language or have traveled, studied, or worked in other countries can be valuable assets to an organization. While an employer may or may not have referenced an international aspect of the position in the job advertisement, some companies have offices or factories in more than one region or country. A candidate who notes multilingual skills may be considered to have a competitive edge over other candidates with similar experience.

If the job for which you are applying notes international communication, it is important to be specific and accurate when you list the language skills you possess.

By being proactive and noting any experiences you have in working with people in other cultures, you may catch the eye of the interviewer even before the interviewing process begins.

1. If you are fluent in another language, create a document that describes the language in which you are proficient, where you received your training, and your level of fluency. Use the heading "Languages Spoken" and your name.

2. If you have limited language proficiency, create a document that says "Limited Language Proficiency" and list each language and your ability to communicate using it. For example, you may have only a limited proficiency in German that could be helpful in a business situation.

3. Update your master portfolio spreadsheet to include your foreign-language skills documentation.

Lesson 12: Portfolio Introduction

After you have collected materials for your portfolio, you are ready to start organizing the content. The first document in your portfolio should be an *introduction* that gives an overall snapshot of who you are. This will set the tone for your presentation, so you want to make a good impression. Tell the reader who you are, your goals, and any relevant biographical information, such as schools attended, titles or certifications earned, or degrees completed. You may want to highlight information by referencing specific sections or page numbers of items in the portfolio.

This document should also include links regarding your online presence. If you are creating an electronic portfolio, provide live links to your pages as well as any pages containing documents of importance.

1. Create a thorough, comprehensive document that introduces yourself, outlines your goals and qualifications, and entices the employer to continue reading your portfolio. Include the heading "Introduction" and your name.

2. Update your master portfolio spreadsheet.

Lesson 13: Presenting the Print Portfolio

You have collected various items for your portfolio, and now it is time to organize the contents. Print the documents that you created as evidence of your abilities, such as your Skills and Talents document. Review the items and select the ones you want to include in your final portfolio. There may be documents that you decide not to use. Opt for quality over quantity. Remember to remove any working documents that you have inserted, such as your objective description.

After you have sorted through the documents and determined the appropriate order, create a divider page for labeling each section that will help organize the material. For example, a page that says *Work Samples* should be placed at the beginning of the section of your portfolio that contains work samples to help give order to your documents.

Prepare a title page. The title page should consist of the word *Portfolio* followed by the phrase *Prepared by* and your full name. Next, create a table of contents. This will help the person reviewing the portfolio locate each item and give a professional appearance to your portfolio.

Conclude your portfolio with a résumé and cover letter. Follow these documents with your list of references and letters of recommendation. Consider adding a photo in this section. Some advisors may suggest against this; however, your photo is probably on your social media pages, so it is not confidential. By including it in your portfolio, it will help the interviewer connect a name and a face when the evaluation process is underway.

Select the folder, binder, or other carrier that will be used to house the print portfolio. You will need multiples because, in most instances, you will leave a portfolio with the interviewer. It is suggested that you initially create two or three at the beginning of the process. As you progress in the job-search process, there will be inevitable changes that you will want to make. If you have created too many initial versions, you may find yourself discarding them.

Remember, a portfolio is a living document and will be updated regularly.

1. Review the documents you have collected. Select the items you want to include in your portfolio. Decide which items you will include, and set aside the documents that you decide are not appropriate for inclusion. Make copies of certificates, diplomas, and other important documents. Keep the originals in a safe place.

2. Organize the documents in the order that you wish them to appear. The title page will appear first. Then, create a table of contents based on your selected order.

3. Place the items in a folder, binder, or other container.

4. Submit the portfolio to an instructor or other person who can give constructive feedback. Review the feedback you received. Make necessary adjustments and revisions.

Lesson 14: Presenting the Electronic Portfolio

After your print portfolio is assembled, decide how to present your electronic portfolio. Just as you did for your print portfolio, review the digital files you have collected. Select the ones you want to include and remove those you do not. Decide how you want to present the materials. For example, you could create an electronic presentation with slides for each section. The slides could have links to documents, videos, graphics, or sound files. Alternatively, you could use a CD or a flash drive to present the material. The Internet also provides ways to help you present and store materials for an electronic portfolio. You could create a personal website with links to various sections. The method you choose should allow the viewer to easily navigate and find items.

Your electronic portfolio will contain documents you created digitally as well as documents that you have in hard-copy format that will be scanned. It will be necessary to decide file formats to use for both types of documents. Before you begin, consider the technology that you might use for creating and scanning documents. You will need access to desktop-publishing software, scanners, cameras, and other digital equipment or software.

For documents that you create, consider using the default format to save the files. For example, you could save letters and essays created in Microsoft Word in the default DOCX format. You could save worksheets created in Microsoft Excel in the default XLSX format. If your presentation will include graphics or video, confirm the file formats that are necessary for each item. Use the appropriate formats as you create the documents.

Hard-copy items will need to be converted to digital format. Portable document format, or PDF, is a good choice for scanned items, such as awards and certificates. Another option is to save all documents as PDF files.

Keep in mind that the person reviewing your electronic portfolio will need programs that open these formats to view your files. Having all of the files in the same format can make viewing them easier for those who need to review your portfolio.

B Punctuation, Capitalization, and Number Expression

Terminal Punctuation

In writing, **punctuation** consists of marks used to show the structure of sentences. Punctuation marks used at the end of a sentence are called *terminal punctuation*. Terminal punctuation marks include periods, question marks, and exclamation points.

Periods

A **period** is a punctuation mark used at the end of a declarative sentence. A *declarative sentence* is one that makes a statement. A period signals to the reader that the expressed thought has ended.

> The final exam will be on May 26.
>
> Alma traveled to Lexington to visit her friend.

A period can be used within a quotation. A period should be placed inside a quotation that completes a statement. If a sentence contains a quotation that does not complete the thought, the period should be placed at the end of the sentence, not the end of the quote.

> Jacobi said, "The project is on schedule."
>
> She told me, "Do not let anyone through this door," and she meant it.

Question Marks

A **question mark** is punctuation used at the end of an interrogative sentence. An *interrogative sentence* is one that asks a question. A question mark can be used after a word or sentence that expresses strong emotion, such as shock or doubt.

> Will the plane arrive on time?
>
> What? Are you serious?

A question mark can be part of a sentence that contains a quotation. Place the question mark inside the quotation marks when the quote asks a question. Place the question mark outside the quotation marks if the entire sentence asks a question.

> Teresa asked, "Will the work be finished soon?"
>
> Did he say, "The sale will end on Friday"?

Exclamation Points

An **exclamation point** is a punctuation mark used to express strong emotion. Exclamation points are used at the end of a sentence or after an interjection that stands alone. An exclamation point can be used at the end of a question rather than a question mark, if the writer wishes to show strong emotion.

> Ouch! Stop hurting me!
>
> Will you ever grow up!

As with other terminal punctuation, an exclamation point can be part of a sentence that contains a quotation. Place the exclamation point inside the quotation marks when the quote expresses the strong emotion. Place the exclamation point outside the quotation marks if the entire sentence expresses the strong emotion.

> All of the students shouted, "Hooray!"
>
> She said, "You are disqualified"!

Internal Punctuation

Punctuation marks used within a sentence are called **internal punctuation**. These marks include commas, dashes, parentheses, semicolons, colons, apostrophes, hyphens, and quotation marks.

Commas

A **comma** is a punctuation mark used to separate elements in a sentence. Commas are used to separate items in a series.

> Apple, pears, or grapes will be on the menu.

A comma is used before a coordinating conjunction that joins two independent clauses.

> The sun rose, and the birds began to sing.

Commas are used to separate a nonrestrictive explanatory word or phrase from the rest of the sentence.

> Gloria's husband, Jorge, drove the car.
> Yes, I will attend the meeting.

A comma is placed before and after an adverb, such as *however* or *indeed*, when it comes in the middle of a sentence.

> Preparing a delicious meal, however, requires using fresh ingredients.

When an adjective phrase contains coordinate adjectives, use commas to separate the coordinate adjectives. The comma takes the place of the word *and*.

> The *long, hot* summer was finally over.

Commas are used to separate words used in direct address. The words can be proper nouns, the pronoun *you*, or common nouns.

> Quon, please answer the next question.
> Everyone, please sit down.

Commas are used to separate elements in dates and addresses. When a date is expressed in the month-day-year format, commas are used to separate the year.

> On December 7, 1941, Japan attacked Pearl Harbor.

When only the month and year or a holiday and year are used, a comma is not needed.

> In January 2010 she retired from her job.

A comma is used after the street address and after the city when an address or location appears in general text.

> Mail the item to 123 Maple Drive, Columbus, OH 43085.

A comma is used to introduce a quotation.

> The speaker attempted to energize the workers by saying, "The only limits are those we put on ourselves."

Dashes and Parentheses

A **dash** is a punctuation mark that separates elements in a sentence or signals an abrupt change in thought. There are two types of dashes: *em dash* and *en dash*. The em dash can be used to replace commas or parentheses to emphasize or set off text. To give emphasis to a break in thought, use an em dash.

> My history teacher—an avid reader—visits the library every week.

The en dash is used as a span or range of numbers, dates, or time.

> We won the baseball game 6–3.
> Barack Obama served as President of the United States from 2009–2017.

Parentheses are punctuation marks used to enclose words or phrases that clarify meaning or give added information. Place a period that comes at the end of a sentence inside the parentheses only when the entire sentence is enclosed in parentheses.

| Deliver the materials to the meeting site (the Polluck Building).

Use parentheses to enclose numbers or letters in a list that is part of a sentence.

| Revise the sentences to correct errors in (1) spelling, (2) punctuation, and (3) capitalization.

Semicolons, Colons, and Apostrophes

A **semicolon** is an internal punctuation mark used to separate independent clauses that are similar in thought. A semicolon can also be used to separate items in a series. Typically, items in a series are separated with commas, but if the serial items include commas, a semicolon should be used to avoid confusion.

| Twelve students took the test; two students passed.
| We mailed packages to Anchorage, AK; Houston, TX; and Bangor, ME.

A **colon** is an internal punctuation mark that introduces an element in a sentence or paragraph.

| The bag contains three items: a book, a pencil, and an apple.

A colon is also used after a phrase, clause, or sentence that introduces a vertical list.

| Follow these steps:

An **apostrophe** is a punctuation mark used to form possessive words. It is most commonly used in conjunction with the letter *s* to show possession. Position of the apostrophe depends on whether the noun is singular or plural. If singular, place the apostrophe between the noun and the *s*. If plural, place the apostrophe after the *s*.

| Akeno's dress was red.
| The students' books were to be put away before the exam.

A **contraction** is a shortened form of a word or term. It is formed by omitting letters from one or more words and replacing them with an apostrophe to create one word—the contraction. An example of a contraction is *it's* for *it is*.

Apostrophes can also be used to indicate that numbers or letters are omitted from words for brevity or writing style.

| Leisure suits were in style in the '60s. (1960s)
| The candidates will meet to discuss activities of the gov't. (government)

Hyphens

A **hyphen** is a punctuation mark used to separate parts of compound words, numbers, or ranges. Compound words that always have a hyphen are called **permanent compounds**.

Some adverbs, such as *on-the-job*, always have hyphens.

| The close-up was blurry.
| My mother-in-law made dinner.
| Their orientation includes on-the-job training.

Compound adjectives have hyphens when they come before the words they modify, but not when they come after them.

| The well-done pot roast was delicious.
| The delicious pot roast was well done.
| These out-of-date books should be thrown away.
| Throw away the books that are out of date.

In some words that have prefixes, a hyphen is used between the prefix and the rest of the word.

| My ex-wife has custody of our children.

When a word is divided at the end of a line of text, a hyphen is used between parts of the word.

| Carter ran down the hall-
| way to answer the door.

Quotation Marks

Quotation marks are used to enclose short, direct quotations and titles of some artistic or written works.

| "Which color do you want," he asked.
| "The Raven" is a poem written by Edgar Allan Poe.

A quotation need not be a complete sentence; it can be a word or a phrase as spoken or written by someone. See the examples that follow.

| When the mayor refers to "charitable giving," does that include gifts to all nonprofit
| organizations?

When writing dialogue, the words of each speaker are enclosed in quotation marks with the appropriate punctuation mark.

| Anna arrived at the office and greeted her coworker, Joan. "Good morning. You're
| getting an early start today."

Chapter or section titles within complete books, movies, or other artistic work are typically shown in quotation marks. The full title of the work is typically italicized.

| "Books and Journals" is the first chapter in *The Chicago Manual of Style*.

Quotation marks are used to enclose words that are meant to show irony.

| Although Connie had the afternoon off, she was too "busy" to help me.
| In a survey of small businesses, one in five managers said their companies are
| "sinking ships."

Capitalization

Capitalization is writing a letter in uppercase (B) rather than lowercase (b). Capital letters signal the beginning of a new sentence and identify important words in titles and headings. Capital letters are also used for proper nouns, for some abbreviations, in personal and professional titles, and for parts of business letters.

A sentence begins with a capital letter. Numbers that begin a sentence should be spelled as words, and the first word should be capitalized.

| Thirty-three students took part in the graduation ceremony.

Capitalize the first, last, and all important words in a heading or title.

| *Gone with the Wind*
| *The Adventure of the Hansom Cabs*

For numbers with hyphens in a heading or title, capitalize both words.

| *Twenty-One Candles*

Do not capitalize articles or prepositions within a heading or title unless it is the first word in the title.

| *The Finest Story in the World*

When a title and subtitle are written together, only the first word of the subtitle is capitalized regardless of the part of speech.

| *Presidential Priorities: College's 10th president outlines three campus goals*

Do not capitalize coordinating conjunctions (*yet*, *and*, *but*, *for*, *or*, and *nor*) in a heading or title.

Pride and Prejudice

Never Marry but for Love

Do not capitalize parts of names that normally appear in lowercase (Ludwig van Beethoven).

His favorite composer is Ludwig van Beethoven.

Capitalize the first word in the salutation for a letter.

Dear Mrs. Stockton:

Capitalize the first word in the complimentary close for a letter.

Sincerely yours,

Proper nouns begin with a capital letter. Recall that a proper noun is a word that identifies a specific person, place, or thing.

Joe Wong is the principal of George Rogers Clark High School.

Capitalize initials used in place of names.

UCLA won the football game.

Capitalize abbreviations that are made up of the first letters of words.

HTML stands for hypertext markup language.

Months and days, as well as their abbreviations, should be capitalized.

Mon. is the abbreviation for Monday.

Abbreviations for names of states and countries should be capitalized.

The price is given in US dollars.

Capitalize abbreviations for directional terms and location terms in street addresses.

She lives at 123 NW Cedar Ave.

Capitalize call letters of a broadcasting company.

My favorite television show is on CBS.

Abbreviations that note an era in time should be in capital letters.

The article included a map of Europe for the year 1200 CE.

Capitalize titles that come before personal names and seniority titles after names.

Sen. Carl Rogers called Mr. Juarez and Dr. Wang.

Mr. Thomas O'Malley, Jr., spoke at the ceremony.

Capitalize abbreviations for academic degrees and other professional designations that follow names.

Jane Patel, LPN, was on duty at the hospital.

Number Expression

Numbers can be expressed as figures or as words. In some cases, as in legal documents and on bank checks, numbers are written in both figures and words. When the two expressions of a number do not agree, readers are alerted to ask for clarification.

Number expression guidelines are not as widely agreed upon as rules for punctuation and capitalization. Follow the guidelines in this section for general writing. If you are writing a research report or an article for a particular group or publication, ask whether there are number expression guidelines you should follow for that item.

Numbers Expressed as Words

In general writing, use words for numbers one through nine.

One dog and three cats sat on the porch.

Use figures for numbers 10 and greater. (See other style guides for exceptions to this guideline.)

| She placed an order for 125 blue ink pens.

When some numbers in a sentence are 9 or less and some are 10 or greater, write all the numbers as figures.

| The box contains 5 books, 10 folders, and 15 pads of paper.

Use words for numbers that are indefinite or approximate amounts.

| About fifty people signed the petition.

Use words for numbers one through nine followed by *million, billion,* and so forth. For numbers 10 or greater followed by *million, billion,* and so forth, use a figure and the word.

| Two million people live in this region.
| By 2016, the population of the United States had grown to over 300 million.

When a number begins a sentence, use words instead of figures. If the number is long when written as words, consider revising the sentence so it does not begin with a number.

| Twenty copies of the report were prepared.

When two numbers come together in a sentence, use words for one of the numbers.

| On the bus, there were 15 ten-year-olds.

Use words for numbers with *o'clock* to express time.

| Come to my house for lunch at eleven o'clock.

Use figures with *a.m.* and *p.m.* to express time.

| The assembly will begin at 9:30 a.m.

To express amounts of money, use figures with a currency sign.

| The total amount is $18,395.40.

Do not use a decimal and two zeros when all dollar amounts in a sentence are whole amounts.

| The charges were $5, $312, and $89.

For an isolated amount less than $1, use figures and the word *cents*.

| Buy a cup of lemonade for 75 cents.

When an amount less than $1 appears with other amounts greater than $1, use figures and dollar signs for all of the numbers.

| The prices were $12.50, $0.89, and $12.45.

For a large, even dollar amount, use the dollar sign, a figure, and a word, such as *million* or *billion*.

| The profits for last year were $5 million.

Days and years in dates should be identified with figures.

| On February 19, 2015, the court was not in session.

Use words for fractions. Note that a hyphen is placed between the words.

| Place one-half of the mixture in the pan.

Use figures for mixed numbers (a whole number and a fraction).

| I bought 3 1/2 yards of red fabric.

When writing a number with decimals, use figures.

| The measurements are 1.358 and 0.878.

Use figures in measurements, such as distance, weight, and percentages.

| We drove 258 miles today.

Glossary

A

academic integrity. Demonstration of honesty and responsibility in completion of academic work and performance as a student. (1)

acronym. Abbreviated words or names formed from the initial letters of other words. (10)

acrostic. Made-up sentence or poem in which the first letter of each line of text spells out a word or message. (10)

active learning. Fully participating in activities that lead to understanding of content or information. (9)

active listening. Act of processing what a person says so the message can be comprehended. (8)

active reading. Processing the words, phrases, and sentences encountered while reading. (7)

annotation. Note or comment added to a document to help explain its contents. (7)

attitude. How personal thoughts or feelings affect a person's outward behavior. (1)

auditory learner. Learner who learns by listening to information. (2)

B

barrier. Anything preventing clear, effective communication. (8)

burnout. Loss of interest due to an overload of work or information. (4)

C

chunking. Memorization method that involves breaking up long strings of information into shorter, more manageable chunks. (10)

citation. Lists the author, title, and publisher of the source; date of publication; and location of the publisher or online address. (12)

comprehend. To grasp, or understand. (6)

conclusion. Writer's summary of what the audience should take away from the report. (13)

context clue. Hint that helps define an unfamiliar word based on the surrounding words in a sentence. (6)

copyright. Acknowledges ownership of a work and specifies that only the owner has the right to sell the work, use it, or give permission for someone else to sell or use it. (12)

cramming. Practice of studying intensely to absorb a large volume of information in a short period of time. (4)

critical-thinking skills. Skills that provide the ability to analyze and interpret a situation and make reasonable judgements and decisions. (1)

D

data. Pieces of information gathered through research. (12)

decision-making. Process of solving a problem or situation. (1)

E

ergonomics. Science of adapting a workstation to fit the needs of a person. (5)

ethics. Moral principles that direct a person's behaviors. (1)

etymology. Origin of a word and the historical development of its meaning. (6)

F

focus. Paying close attention to something. (1)

focus group. Small group of people with which the interviewer leads a discussion to gather answers to a set of questions. (12)

G

goal. Something to be achieved in a specified time period. (3)

goal setting. Process of deciding what needs to be achieved and defining the period of time in which to achieve it. (3)

Note: The number in parenthesis following each definition indicates the chapter in which the term can be found.

H

heading. Words and phrases introducing a section of a text. (13)

hearing. Physical process. (8)

I

infringement. Any use of copyrighted material without permission. (12)

integrity. Honesty of a person's actions. (1)

intellectual property. Something that comes from a person's mind, such as an idea, an invention, or a process. (12)

K

kinesthetic. Bodily movement. (2)

kinesthetic-tactile learner. Learner who learns by performing hands-on or physical activities. (2)

L

learning. Behavior that enables an individual to acquire information. (10)

learning style. Methods an individual prefers and finds most effective for processing and absorbing information. (2)

listening. Intellectual process that combines hearing with evaluating. (8)

long-term memory. Storage of information for an extended period of time. (10)

M

meditation. Practice of focusing one's mind for a period of time as a method of relaxation or for religious purposes. (14)

memorize. Recite material word-for-word. (10)

memory. Part of the mind where information is encoded, stored, and retrieved. (10)

memory retrieval. Accessing information from long-term memory when it is needed. (10)

mnemonic. Any learning technique that helps a person remember something. (10)

morals. Individual's ideas of what is right and wrong. (1)

N

negative reinforcement. Occurs when an individual talks with someone who encourages their negative attitudes. (14)

note taking. Process of writing key information from a lecture, text, or other sources on paper or a digital device. (9)

P

piracy. Unethical and illegal copying or downloading of software, files, or other protected material. (12)

plagiarism. Claiming another person's material as one's own, which is both unethical and illegal. (1)

primary research. First-hand research conducted by the writer in preparation for writing a report. (12)

prior knowledge. Experience and information a person already possesses. (7)

prioritize. Determine the order of importance in which tasks should be completed. (3)

procrastination. Putting off a task until a later time. (3)

progressive muscle relaxation. Relaxation of different muscle groups over a short period of time. (14)

public domain. Material with no owner that can be used without permission. (12)

Q

qualitative data. Pieces of information that provide insight into how people think about a particular topic. (12)

quantitative data. Facts and figures from which conclusions can be drawn. (12)

R

read for detail. Read all words and phrases, consider their meanings, and determine how they combine with other elements to convey ideas. (7)

readability. Measure of how easy it is for the audience to understand your writing. (13)

reading comprehension. Ability to understanding what has been read. (6)

recommendation. Actions the writer believes the reader should take. (13)

representative sampling. Group including a cross section of the entire population the writer is targeting. (12)

research. Process of investigation for the purpose of establishing facts and drawing conclusions. (12)

research paper. Formal report that involves extensive research, critical thinking, and analysis of a position taken by the writer. (13).

rote learning. Remembering though repetition. (10)

S

scan. Quickly glance through material to find specific information. (7)

secondary research. Data someone else already assembled and recorded. (12)

self-assess. Evaluate what a person has learned without the outcome of a grade. (11)

self-confidence. Being certain and secure about one's own abilities and judgement. (1)

self-talk. Practice of talking to oneself, either silently or aloud. (1)

shorthand. Method of rapid writing using abbreviations and symbols. (9)

short-term memory. Where information is retained and recalled for a brief moment without rehearsal. (10)

skill. Something an individual does well. (1)

skim. Quickly glance through material to get an overview. (7)

SMART goal. Goal that is specific, measurable, attainable, realistic, and timely. (3)

soft skills. Skills used to communicate and work well with others. (1)

SQ3R. Reading strategy to help readers retain written information, also called *SQRRR*. (7)

stress. Body's reaction to increased demands or dangerous situations. (14)

stress management. Variety of strategies used to cope with stress and limit its effects. (14)

stress-management skills. Skills that enable an individual to identify and control stress. (14)

study environment. Place where textbooks are read, school materials reviewed, assignments completed, and test preparation takes place. (5)

study skills. Strategies a person applies to learning. (1)

study time. Block of minutes or hours designated to complete homework, read materials for class, or work on other assignments that must be accomplished according to a specific time schedule. (4)

summarize. Active listening technique that entails writing or thinking about the main points a person has read or heard. (8)

survey. Set of questions posed to a group of people to determine how that group thinks, feels, or acts. (12)

synonym. Word with a similar meaning. (6)

T

table of contents. Lists the major sections and subsections within a report with page numbers. (13)

tactile. Sense of touch. (2)

time management. Practice of organizing time and work assignment to increase personal efficiency. (3)

tone. Impression of the overall content of the message. (13)

transferable skills. Skills that help an individual find a job, perform well in the workplace, and gain success in a job or career. (1)

V

visual learner. Learner who learns by seeing information or observing things. (2)

vocabulary development. Process people use to increase the number of words with which they are familiar. (6)

voracious. Excessively eager. (6)

Index